The Art of Power and Control Selling

The Art of Power
and
Control Selling

The Salesman's Bible

Calvin Hill

Exposition Press
Hicksville, New York

FIRST EDITION

© 1980 by Calvin Hill

ISBN 0-682-49547-6

Printed in the United States of America

This book is dedicated to the millions of salespeople selling to the public in every part of the world, and to my son, Calvin Hill, Jr., whom I love very much—remember with power and control all things are possible

Contents

7

The Art of Power and Control Selling

Introduction

To the millions of salespeople selling for thousands of companies: this book is for you salespeople on a draw or commission, who sell directly to the customer, and who do not want to be merely average.

The Art of Power and Control Selling will probably be the most effective book on sales you will ever read. If you follow this method, it will do exactly what it says it will do. You will exert power and you will have control. In sales, that adds up to dollars and cents.

As an added bonus, when you learn the methods this book expounds, you will have more confidence in your ability than ever before, more effectiveness as a salesperson than ever before, and more respect for yourself as a dynamic, productive human being than you've ever had before. In addition, you will have more assurance to meet the customer head-on in battle and come off the battlefield victorious more often than ever before.

1

Confusion: The Salesman's Mortal Enemy

If there ever was one word referring to a state of mind that has lost more sales, created more problems, and cost salespeople almost as much money as the national debt, that word is "confusion." Remember that word "confusion." We have all heard that word used in different contexts. You've probably heard someone say all of the following: (1) "I'm so confused, I don't know whether I'm coming or going," (2) "I got lost because I got confused about the directions," (3) "Your explanation is about the most confusing thing I have ever heard," (4) "That person creates confusion wherever she goes," and (5) "Why do you look so confused? Don't you understand?"

As you can see, no matter how that word is used, it means there is a problem. If I wanted to expand this subject, I could go on to say that confusion has caused serious misunderstandings among people. It has brought about divorces, feuds, lawsuits, splits in families, and breakups of long-time friendships. Confusion has caused murders. Wars have been caused by confusion and have brought great destruction of property and the death of thousands. I don't mean to belabor you with sad facts. I want you to be able to understand all the facts about confusion and its ramifications. Understanding that confusion, for any reason, can cost you money and lost sales is of paramount importance.

You must understand that the most intelligent and most experienced people cannot make a decision when they are confused. So, rather than try to make a decision to purchase any product or service in that state of mind, a customer simply says no. You've probably heard the saying, "When in doubt, do nothing." You could very easily substitute a word and say, "When confused, do nothing." Don't use one hundred words when fifty would have been sufficient. Keep things direct and simple. The shortest distance between two points is a straight line.

You must understand that the customer knows what he is about, his job, his environment, his family, and his friends. The world you are introducing the customer to in selling your product or service is almost always unfamiliar to him. In other words, he doesn't know or understand your business.

This customer may deal with you only once a year or once every five years. This unfamiliarity leaves a vacuum that invites confusion. It depends upon what you say and how you say it to either fill that void with your power and control, or fill that vacuum with so much confusion that the customer's mind is hopelessly deadlocked and a decision is impossible. But, you see, you also have the golden opportunity to take control of the customer's thoughts and actions, and guide him down the road to a successful sale for you. Whether you fill that vacuum with your power and control depends upon what you say and how you say it. *The Art of Power and Control Selling* teaches you what to say and how to say it to get the financial rewards you seek.

You must keep this fact uppermost in mind: the spoken word is the most powerful force on earth. We all know the only difference between man and animal is man's ability to think and reason. But without the spoken word, that difference could not have been exploited in man's favor. Let us go back in time to find out how the state of confusion began, and how it became a part of the American consumer's daily life.

After the major upheaval in peoples' lives caused by World War II was over, people settled down to buy the houses, cars, appliances, and whatever else had not been plentiful or wasn't even being produced. When all the soldiers came back home, they started families and began having children in record numbers. Life was relatively simple then. Inflation was so low, it wasn't even a factor. All the industries that had given over to producing arms for the war effort were converted back to producing civilian consumer goods. The American consumer had a voracious appetite fueled by years of doing without. Prices were low. The economy was booming. There was a great sense of serenity and relief throughout the land. Why not? The war was finally over. Great expectations of peace and prosperity filled the country. People felt they were in control of their own destinies. Crises like Korea, Vietnam, race riots, lack of faith in one's government, skyrocketing inflation, and the energy crunch were just waiting for their time to appear, to spread confusion and fear the width and breadth of this land.

Back then, people seemed to know where they were going and how they would get there. After the big war was over, people felt there would be nothing but blue skies and sunshine for years and years to come. This was not to be. The American consumer would eventually doubt his own confidence in himself, his government, and the American way of life. American consumers were to receive shock after shock, after shock, after shock, until they were literally numb. If you were to describe today's consumer as dazed, shocked, and in a state of confusion, you could not give a better description.

We are getting ahead of our story. The first shock came in Korea in 1949, after we were pulled into that so-called police action or undeclared war, or whatever you want to call it. The killing of young American boys, many too young to drink, was shocking, to say the least. The most tragic aspect of the whole bloody mess is that nothing was gained. But something was lost. This country had not won a war for the first time in its history.

In 1965, something happened that brought confusion and fear to the white American consumer. Black people, sick and tired of decades and decades of discrimination, prejudice, and mistreatment, began to riot in the major American cities, threatening to burn them to the ground. There were marches, demonstrations, and violence on both sides. A humble black preacher from Atlanta by the name of Martin Luther King began to prick the nation's conscience with his nonviolent methods. Laws were passed and the black man was determined that he would be a second-class citizen no longer. He reasoned this was his country, too; he wanted to share in its fruits.

We now come to the third shock. When the racial situation in this country began to cool down, seven thousand miles away in a small Asian country called Vietnam, which most Americans had never heard of before, things were heating up and soon became white-hot. This war developed into the most divisive issue since the Civil War. The younger generation opposed the older generation; the hawks opposed the doves. Some of these wounds still have not healed. This war probably created more confusion, more frustration, and more downright anger than ever before. This war brought about more change in America than anything in the last one hundred years.

Before Americans could digest the ending of the Vietnam War, this country was shocked for a fourth time by the resignation of the vice-president and the first resignation ever of an American president. This was brought about by deceit, shady dealings, outright lies, and the commission of crimes that sent some of the most important men in government to jail. Nixon himself escaped through the pardon of the man he named to succeed him. There was revelation after revelation of dirty dealings, underhandedness, cheating, and lying by the very leaders Americans had chosen to lead them and uphold the law. The people's disenchantment and loss of faith was immediate and massive.

With the massive spending for the Vietnam War as a catalyst, inflation started upward by leaps and bounds, causing shock number five. Prices on goods and services began to increase in one year as much as they had in the previous three or four years combined. Old people on fixed incomes and low-income people really suffered from the squeeze. They became afraid and confused by what was happening to them. The white-collar and blue-collar workers found their incomes no longer kept pace with skyrocketing inflation. What is so terribly confusing to the consumer is that no one seems to know what to do about it.

You who are in sales, make no mistake about it. We are dealing with the most confused, most frustrated, most resentful consumer in the history of this country. The pathetic thing about today's consumer is that he feels completely powerless and helpless, and feels he no longer has control over his life. In between the unpopular wars, the race riots, the loss of faith in one's own government, and the skyrocketing inflation, there have been deep recessions with millions out of work. Crime is running rampant. Our prisons are overflowing. Add to this declining morals and our loss of prestige around the world. And then came the cruelest blow of all: an energy crunch with a full-blown energy shortage. We had to line up for hours to get a tankful of gas, and prices have gone over a dollar a gallon. Who's to blame? The consumer blames the big oil companies' insatiable greed. The big oil companies blame the OPEC countries' greed. The OPEC countries blame the American consumer for using and wasting too much. I must admit, I'm pretty confused. Just think of how confused the poor American consumer must be.

The Art of Power and Control Selling will teach you how to take the confusion out of selling and closing. Once you have learned this method, the likelihood of letting a customer become confused is almost nil. You, as a salesperson, hold the absolute power of whether a customer does or does not become confused. You must realize what a tremendous and dynamic asset this can be. Your ability to do this would be the difference between success or failure. My associates and students have called this Hill's Law: LET NOT THY CUSTOMER BECOME CONFUSED.

2

How to Become
Mentally, Psychologically, and
Emotionally Tough

There are many people who have the talent to succeed, but not the mental toughness. Remember this phrase "mental toughness." It will become one of the most important building blocks in your climb to success. I repeat again, "mentally tough." Once you have learned how to be mentally tough, you can literally break through a brick wall. Being mentally tough in the art of power and control selling will bring you unprecedented financial success in your field. It will also have a very positive effect on your personal life with acquaintances, friends, and loved ones.

When you have become mentally tough, you will experience a great surge of mental strength. You will begin to deal with other people from a position of strength rather than weakness. You will even amaze yourself, and others may hold you in awe when you display this newly found power. You can develop mental toughness to any degree you may choose. You can develop a will of iron that will break down any barrier standing in your way.

I am sure we have all known people who seem to have all of the ingredients—the intelligence, the talent—but they somehow never quite seem to succeed. Along comes another person who seems to have none of these qualities but somehow has found the magic formula for success. What is the difference between these two people? The one who seems to have all the successful qualities does not succeed. The one who seems to have none of the above qualities succeeds. The difference is mental toughness. Mental toughness gives you the will to succeed. This will to succeed can sweep away all the obstacles, problems, and barriers that stand in your way.

Am I saying mental toughness is more important than talent? I give an unqualified yes. Mental toughness is more important than talent. But if you have the talent and develop mental toughness, you can be much more successful.

What is the meaning of this magical phrase and how do I acquire it? Mental toughness is a combination of desire, an insatiable need for success, and a driving ambition to be good at whatever you do. This drive need not be an all-consuming ambition, because we all are not made to be full of ambition

all of the time. Having some ambition to do well
is necessary. Another ingredient is the willingness
to work, in other words, to put forth a reasonable
effort.

I am going to give you a step-by-step procedure
to become mentally tough. To make sure you understand the formula for becoming mentally tough and
the procedures by which this can be done, I will
discuss the ingredients and how they are used.

DESIRE

The desire to be a success in our business lives,
our family lives, and our social lives is within all of
us. For the time being, let's concentrate on your
business life. When we improve your money-making
capabilities, and you are able to do this with less
frustration and less mental strain and pressure than
before, it's amazing how much your family life and
social life will improve. To be surrounded by this
stimulating set of circumstances is the beginning of
your road to success in your chosen sales profession.
This desire must be changed from mere thoughts
to usable, effective mental energy. Desire is going
to be the catalyst to make things happen.

Your desires will become your goals. When
desiring an income, don't desire a $25,000 or

$30,000 income. Desire a $75,000 or $80,000 income, and don't only desire this high income—say out loud that you are going to have it. Say it twenty, thirty, forty times, even fifty times a day, one right after the other. Start off saying it softly and deliberately. As you begin repeating these phrases, raise your voice each time you repeat the words until you reach a crescendo. Put power into your words because you mean exactly what you say and you are serious about what you say. Put anger in your voice as if to say, "What customer would have the audacity to keep me from reaching my goal?" I want you to repeat this desire and any other desires you may have. Repeat these desires many times a day. You must do it with power, with seriousness, and with anger. Make the same statement, substituting a house for money. Don't desire a $50,000 house; desire a $100,000 house or a $150,000 house. Say it out loud, say it often, raising your voice each time. Say it with power, with seriousness, and with anger. You will say to yourself, "Nothing—but nothing—is going to stand in my way." Whatever goals you set for yourself, use the same procedures, substituting whatever word you want. Always, but always, use the same procedures. I repeat again, say it with power, seriousness, and anger.

When desire is developed to a certain degree, it creates a need. When nurtured, this need will become an insatiable need for success, a need that only success can satisfy. Let's stop and define the word "success." Success does not have to be a $100,000 income or a $200,000 house. Success can be doubling your present income. It can be moving from a $40,000 house to a $75,000 house. It can mean you are able to provide for your family more adequately. Success can be a cabin cruiser or a trip around the world. As we stated, everybody has his own meanings for success. The need for success is now a daily thought that has been cataloged in your subconscious. It can be recalled to action at any time. We are going to program ourselves to achieve the mental toughness we desire.

Rodney had been selling for six years with just moderate success. His life in sales was filled with a great deal of frustration. He never seemed to get it all together. Rodney has a wife and two kids. His wife worked at a local hospital, making a moderate income. Their combined income was $26,000 last year, which is not too great, considering today's rate of inflation. Rodney seemed at times on the verge of breaking out of the mold of mediocrity, but never seemed to have the mental stamina to do so. Nor did Rodney know what to do to acquire the mental stamina. The mind must be trained to acquire stamina to perform feats of endurance, just like the body. Just as a marathon runner cannot succeed if his body is not physically tough, a salesman cannot succeed if his mind is not mentally tough.

Remember the procedures that I gave you earlier in this chapter. Repeating your desires with power, seriousness, and anger will play a major part in your becoming mentally tough. When these desires have become insatiable needs, you will have come a long way on the road to becoming mentally tough.

If you follow what *The Art of Power and Control Selling* tells you to do, it is almost impossible not to get the desired effect, unless you yourself choose not to make it work. I will repeat that statement. It is almost impossible for you not to become mentally tough unless you choose not to be.

The other ingredient that will assist you in becoming mentally tough is work. Without hard work, nothing can be accomplished. After repeating your desires thirty, forty to fifty times a day for one and one-half to two months, you will feel an insatiable need to accomplish the things you desire. You then go to work, working with dedication and single-mindedness. Whatever methods or prospecting you use to get business, double the amount of time you spent before, double the amount of work for prospecting. This will not be difficult because the strong desires and the insatiable need to succeed begin to drive you. Mental toughness is starting to take hold.

Double the number of prospects you had been seeing before. You will be able to accomplish this because you will not need to spend as much time selling the prospect as before. You will not be as tired because most of the mental struggling and pressure you've experienced in the past will be eliminated. (The next chapter will tell you why.)

The strong urge to work hard will become a part of your day. The will to work harder will become easier as you become mentally tougher. You will find yourself able to accomplish twice as much in half the time. You must always remember that the most important asset a salesperson has is time. When you waste time, you are wasting money. When you become mentally tough, you will work with such dedication that wasting time will become a thing of the past. Let all the people around you waste as much time as they wish. You are now marching to a different drummer. The power and mental stamina you acquire will amaze you. As your mental toughness grows, your income will grow. As your mental toughness grows, your confidence will grow. You are on that dynamic merry-go-round that will guarantee success in your chosen field.

I am going to explain how something that seems

so magical happens and makes you so mentally tough, you can break down the sales barriers in your particular business as if they were matchsticks. You will actually program yourself to build the mental toughness we have been talking about. If you use the procedures I have given you, you cannot fail to achieve the desired results.

There is a certain amount of psychology involved in any change in a person's mental outlook and his thoughts about himself. It can be the change in one's desire, the change in one's needs, or even the mental stamina or ability for one to work harder and be more effective than ever before. Let's leave all the psychological terms that could be used and repeated to the psychiatrist and psychologist.

I am neither, but as a commissioned salesman myself who has made a six-figure income in a business that less than one-half of one percent of the salesmen in my field have ever done (refer to my taxable income, $102,000, for 1978), I know these methods work successfully—not because I say so, but because I have used them on the battlefield of salesmanship myself. I have met the enemy on the salesperson's field of battle and have come away victorious. By following the procedures in *The Art of Power and Control Selling*, you will be victorious, too.

You will hear the term "mentally tough" many times throughout the rest of this book. This relatively simple-sounding phrase is one of the premier building blocks on which *The Art of Power and Control Selling* is based. Read this again and again. if necessary, to fully understand the procedures you must follow to become mentally tough. The methods I am advocating are not theory or hearsay. These methods have been tested and proven in the trenches and on the battlefield of sales and in the sales arena.

Salespeople are the frontline troops, and just as in war, you must have the most modern and effective weapons available if you are going to win.

3

The Art of Power Selling
through Control

If any of you reading this book are making eighty thousand dollars a year or more and find your job so easy and satisfying it's like a picnic, then you don't need this course. There is nothing that I could do for you that you are not already doing for yourself. You are doing just fine the way you are. I am not one to tamper with success. You should give this book to someone who needs it more than you do, because obviously you don't.

Now, I'm going to ask you a question. Would you like to increase your income thousands of dollars a year and spend less effort doing it? I knew before I asked that that was a loaded question. Now, let me be a little more profound, direct, and a bit more realistic. In reading this book, if you had the opportunity to actually increase your earning power thousands of dollars a year, with less effort, by making yourself a more effective salesperson, would you take advantage of it? These are the answers that actually count or mean something.

I know you must be asking the question: What can *The Art of Power and Control Selling* do for me? Well, these are the steps you will be taught in this book. *The Art of Power and Control Selling* WILL TEACH YOU:

1. How to take control the minute you greet the customer and increase that control as you go along.
2. How to give commands the customer will automatically follow.
3. How to condition the customer's mind and make him receptive.
4. How to immediately make the customer like and respect you.
5. How to make the customer think that you think and feel just as he does.
6. How to phrase your sales pitch to make it so effective the sale is almost automatic.
7. How to answer objections in one sentence.
8. How to ask questions that always call for "yes" answers.
9. Knowing exactly when to close.
10. Knowing the exact words to use when you close.

You must admit that's promising quite a bit. It's almost like saying *The Art of Power and Control Selling* will teach you how to sell so effectively from start to finish that it's almost automatic. Well, you know something? I stand on record and say that *The Art of Power and Control Selling* will do exactly what it promises, and more. And you probably wonder: what do I mean by more? I mean, more confidence in your ability than you ever had before; more effectiveness as a salesperson than you've ever had before; more respect for yourself as a dynamic, productive human being than you've ever had before; and more self-assurance to meet the customer head-on in battle and come off the field of battle victorious more often than ever before.

You might wonder how to accomplish all these wonderful things. We simply feel that we have the most modern and effective sales course ever devised. *The Art of Power and Control Selling* was created specifically to cope with today's modern buyer. Today's consumer is burdened with a great amount of fear and anxiety, mixed with frustration and a feeling of utter hopelessness. Will we all be drowned in a sea of inflation that no one seems to be able to control? Will inflation destroy the quality of life as we know it today? Many Americans are asking that question. The American consumer is more afraid and more confused than ever in the history of this country. The energy crisis is no longer a myth. It is a painful and frustrating reality that could deal the final blow to the consumers' confidence in their country and their leaders' ability to lead them out of the inflationary jungle. The American consumer is also angry, probably angrier than he has ever been before. He doesn't know who to blame, because everybody is blaming everybody else. This situation just makes things more confused. Adding to the confusion are the outlandish and idiotic advertisements you see, hear, or read. Do you really know what cars are best, or what insurance plan is best, or what house is the best buy? The advertisements say they are all the best, which can't be true. I'm confused; just think of how confused the poor customer must be.

Today's customer is also more intelligent than ever before. He's able to go places and see things that people of past generations only dreamed about. He's more informed than ever before. He knows what's going on in any part of the world seconds after it happens. Tell me, how can a person be more intelligent than ever before and more informed than ever before, and at the same time be more confused and feel more powerless than ever before? It's very confusing, but that's today's customer!

We feel that to do a good selling job today, you must have complete control of the customer. Without control, you're facing a closed mind, and selling develops into a tug-of-war between the customer and the salesman that is exhausting and frustrating, and the salesman usually loses. *The Art of Power and Control Selling* teaches you how to take control of the customer the minute you greet him. It teaches you how to increase your control as you go along so that when you finish your sales presentation, the customer is literally eating out of your hand.

It does not matter what product or service you are selling. You will find *The Art of Power and Control Selling* the most effective and helpful course you have ever had. This sales training course teaches you how to control the customer's thoughts, actions, and reactions. Remember, the same Mr. Smith that bought his car from Jim bought his house from Joe, bought his boat from Bill, bought his home improvement from George, and bought his insurance from Bob. Even though the products or services are different and even the sales terminology and techniques change from business to business, Mr. Smith does not; he remains the same person, no matter what he's buying. *The Art of Power and Control Selling* teaches you how to take control of Mr. Smith. At the end of some procedures, I will ask you to bring to mind information or sales terminology that is familiar or related to your particular product or service.

Picture two men with saws. One has a handsaw and the other a chain saw. The man who is using the handsaw is ambitious, not afraid of work. He's up early every morning and out on the job. He's just about the hardest-working guy you've ever seen. He huffs and puffs and just knocks himself out all day long. At the end of the day, he has accomplished very little, and he's plumb tuckered out. On the other hand, the man with the chain saw just breezes through the work—doesn't sweat, cuts ten times as much wood, and is refreshed at the end of the day. The guy with the handsaw reminds me of great many salespeople who are trying to get today's job done with yesterday's old-fashioned and out-of-date methods. They need a power assist, just like the guy with the chain saw; and *The Art of Power and Control Selling* is going to be that assist.

You've all probably seen or heard of Arthur Miller's classic tragedy. It's a play called *Death of a Salesman*. The play ran for years on Broadway and was made into a movie which won several Academy Awards. There is one line in the play that stands out in my mind. It's about a salesman who was riding on "a smile and a shoeshine." He ends his life a tragic, beaten, and pathetic figure, because the days of getting by on a smile and a shoeshine are over. It's like the five-cent cup of coffee—gone . . . never to return.

You salesmen with experience: how many times have you had this happen to you? You go to work, hoping and praying it's going to be a good day. The first customer you get that day is impossible to sell; while not buying, he has taken the wind out of your sails—made you sweat and pushed you to the wall. You begin to think there must be an easier way to make a living. By the time you get home, you are so frustrated, you begin to holler at the wife and kids for no apparent reason, or suffer periods of depression that can last for days. This can sometimes bring about a serious drinking problem. You also begin to think about a regular, nine-to-five job, where that machine you operate, or that clerk's job you get, won't talk back and give you ulcers.

What you needed most desperately was the proper weapons, or, in this case, training to fight the battle successfully. *The Art of Power and Control Selling* will give you more confidence and more effectiveness than you ever had before.

Now, in going through your sales presentation, keep in mind that you begin to close the sale the minute you greet the customer. Every step is planned and carefully executed from beginning to end. You are going to learn from this course that rather than react to the customer, you are going to have the customer react to you. You know, most salesmen don't know what they are going to say after they greet a customer. Their conception of selling is hearing what the customer thinks, answering all his questions at length, and trying to overcome all of his objections at length, which can sometimes take hours. Then they hope they overcame enough of the customer's objections and the customer might decide to buy. So, we have that tug-of-war again, and the salesman usually loses.

Or, he might be the kind who thinks that by being overly courteous and pleasant, the customer might be charmed into buying. He thinks if he keeps smiling his best smile, the customer will think, "This salesman seems like a nice guy; I'll buy from him."

Do you remember that line in Arthur Miller's play about riding on a smile and a shoeshine? It simply doesn't work anymore. The public is too confused and is getting more confused every day. With *The Art of Power and Control Selling*, you will know exactly what to say every minute, with no embarrassing periods of silence that give the customer a chance to raise doubts or begin to think negatively. *The Art of Power and Control Selling* will make your job much easier and not leave you exhausted and completely frustrated at the end of the day. I repeat: you will know exactly what steps to take every minute of the sale. You will control your customers and sales completely, and not have them control you. You will get the job done in one-half the time and with such ease, you will be amazed!

Any new knowledge you gain must be learned. The learning process involves repetition; in other words, hearing or reading some material over and over again until the mind makes its own recording through the memory process.

The Art of Power and Control Selling is constructed so that you go from one step to the next without any hesitation. You don't want to give the customer a chance to think for himself because the customer only confuses himself, which makes your job three times as hard, and you often end up losing the customer.

We are not so naive as to say you can prohibit or stop a customer from thinking, period. However, we do believe in taking control of a customer by the method you will be taught in *The Art of Power and Control Selling.* The customer's thoughts will be in reaction to your control and to what you are telling him, which, in either case, will bring the customer further under your control.

I feel I must say this before going further: before

any instruction can be meaningful and helpful to you, you must not only understand the motives for each individual step or procedure, but you must understand the whole, in relation to the parts.

To try and make this crystal clear, I will use this example: picture two glasses full of water. One glass is labeled "Customer's Control." The other glass is labeled "Salesman's Control." You are, in effect, picking up the customer's glass, pouring out his water (or his control), and leaving his glass empty. You then pour the water from your own glass into the customer's empty glass. There sits the customer's glass, filled with your water or control. Each procedure in *The Art of Power and Control Selling* first empties the customer's glass and then fills the empty glass, step by step.

So, concentrate on the procedures as you read them, for we believe, beyond a shadow of a doubt, that *The Art of Power and Control Selling* will increase your income thousands of dollars a year. You will have more confidence, more effectiveness, and your job will be more pleasant and satisfying when you learn the procedures of this course and execute them the same way with every customer until it becomes automatic. I repeat, you will say the same things the same way to every customer you meet. You will know your lines so well that you will be able to repeat them in your sleep.

Who would be more believable? One who is ad-libbing, or a craftsman who has practiced and rehearsed his lines and can draw out of his audience the reactions he desires by what he says, the way he says it, and the tone of voice when saying it? The audience reacts to him, not vice versa. You are going to have the customer react to you and what you say, not the other way around. You will practice what you will say, how you will say it, and the tone of voice you will use until they are orchestrated into a symphony of successful selling.

I use the words "learning lines" as an actor would learn lines. Selling is basically acting. In other words, when you sell, you are acting out a part to influence another person to do what you want them to do, meaning buying whatever you are selling. *The Art of Power and Control Selling,* in essence, teaches you the most effective things to say, the most effective way to say them, and the most effective tone of voice to say them in. We advise you to say the same thing every time, the same way every time. I could simplify the reasoning by saying, "Practice makes perfect."

THE FIRST STEP YOU WILL LEARN IS TO TAKE CONTROL OF THE CUSTOMER THE MINUTE YOU GREET HIM AND GIVE HIM COMMANDS HE WILL AUTOMATICALLY FOLLOW. Taking control of the customer the minute you greet him is very important, if not all-important! You must remind yourself again and again just how important taking control of the customer can be.

You might compare it to a key. With this key and other keys you will find in *The Art of Power and Control Selling*, you are going to unlock the customer's mind and his wallet and extract his willingness to buy and the money to buy it with. Remember, imprint this upon your mind forever: without control, you have nothing, and with control, you have everything! Taking control of the customer the minute you greet him is one of those keys.

When you take control and give commands, the customer will automatically follow your lead. Greet the customer with a firm handshake. Smile, look him straight in the eye, and introduce yourself in a firm and authoritative voice. I repeat: a firm and authoritative voice. If you are in a business where you can have the customer follow you, do so at once.

You begin immediately getting the customer used to following commands. With power and authority, you command the customer to follow you. This will be the first of many commands that you will give him throughout the sale. You'll notice I didn't say "ask," I said "command." That's exactly what I mean: command! If your field is

such that you cannot command a customer to follow you—for instance, if you are an insurance man
or any salesman who sells inside the house—if you
are sitting in the living room, command the customer to sit at the dining room table, or command
the customer's wife to join you. Any command you
think of that is appropriate, have him follow. You
want to give the customer as many commands as
possible after introducing yourself. The reason for
doing this is to immediately condition the customer's
mind to follow your commands so that he will con-
tinue to do so throughout the sale . . . automatically.

To explain why this approach works, let's analyze the psychology behind the initial approach.
Two things that people respect most are power and
authority. The more confused people become, the
more they yield to power and authority. Power and
authority are the very foundation of this sales training course. We not only intend to enhance your
sales, business, and moneymaking capabilities, we
also intend to enhance your nonbusiness side by
making this philosophy of power, authority, and
control a total way of life. Once you have mastered
the techniques explained in this book, you will find
yourself operating from a position of strength rather
than weakness. You will also find people being
drawn to you, as if by a magnet.

I cannot stress too much the importance of a

firm and authoritative voice. Unless all procedures in this book are handled in a firm and authoritative voice, it will not matter how well you execute these procedures. Their effectiveness would be nil. You will hear me repeat these words "a firm and authoritative voice" many times throughout this book.

The reason that a firm and authoritative voice is so vitally important is that it lets the customer know, from beginning to end, beyond a shadow of a doubt, who is in control.

Many of you may not speak in a firm and authoritative voice, but this can be learned with practice. For an exercise to strengthen your vocal chords, count from one to one hundred in a firm voice, two or three times a day. This voice exercise will only take a few minutes a day. It must be done religiously until your voice has a firm and authoritative sound. And once you have reached that point through my voice exercises, the voice will take care of itself. And to explain further, the sound of an authoritative voice is a voice that sounds as if it is giving orders or commands.

Some of you reading this book may have an authoritative voice, but it is not being controlled. Remember, the human voice is the most important part of a human being's anatomy. It is of such importance in the art of power and control selling that it cannot be stressed too much or too strongly.

Voice control is the most effective control that one human being can exert on another. To give you dramatic evidence of this statement, you can repeat a line of dialogue and it means nothing. An actor can take that same line and make someone cry or make someone angry or sad, or make him laugh or feel pain, just by the way he says it. Your voice and how you use it will determine whether you will be a failure or a success in sales. It is not only what you say but how you say it. I repeat again, it is not what you say that will make you successful, but how you say it. It's the way you use your voice that will give you the power, authority, and control for success.

You must consider every customer an adversary with whom you are locked in mortal combat. The most successful plan of battle in every war ever fought is to smash the enemy's defenses and render him helpless and vulnerable.

A customer has his own particular defenses. We shall call these defenses "reasons for not buying." The customer will not buy because he does not have an open mind, or because he does not trust you or believe you are telling him the truth. He may feel that you are not being fair because he asked a question or raised an objection that you did not answer to his satisfaction. All of these are a customer's defenses or reasons for not buying. You will learn how to break down these and all other defenses a customer may have and bring him further under your control.

NOW THAT YOU HAVE TAKEN CONTROL OF THE CUSTOMER AND HAVE BEGUN TO GIVE HIM COMMANDS, THE NEXT STEP IN THE AUTOMATIC SALES TRAINING COURSE IS TO LEARN HOW TO OPEN THE CUSTOMER'S MIND, MAKE HIM RECEPTIVE, AND MAKE HIM IMMEDIATELY LIKE AND RESPECT YOU.

Whenever a customer wants to buy something, many things run through his mind, such as the kind of product or service that is being offered with the features he "thinks" he would want. These include style, model, color, extra equipment, special features, present benefits, future benefits, safety, beauty, convenience, terms, etc. You'll notice I said "thinks" he wants. This is because the customer usually does not know enough about your business to know what is best for him or what would be most effective for his needs. But there is one thing he is very positive about: he wants and demands the best possible deal or price he can get anywhere in the country, or he simply won't buy what you are selling. You can't blame him, because money doesn't come easily. And, as strange as it may seem, everyone thinks he works twice as hard as the next guy for his paycheck. He thinks about the sweat, the hardships he endured, or the days, months, and years it took him to acquire this money. He's going to try and spend it just as hard.

Speaking of good deals, you've heard people say, "I felt it was a pretty good deal, so I bought." Or, "It sounded like a good buy and I bought." "It was something we needed and the price seemed reasonable."

You want to make the customer think he is getting the best deal he can possibly get anywhere. A good deal is relative; it's all in the mind. You could sell a customer a product or service at a 100 percent profit, and if he's convinced it's a good deal, he'll buy.

You could try to sell the same product or service to someone else at your actual cost or below, and the customer will not buy because he is not convinced it's a good deal.

The most damaging and deadly weapon a customer can use against a salesman is the fact that he can shop and compare prices, or bid one price against the other.

So, to overcome this problem, we are going to open the customer's mind and make him receptive, because an open mind is like an unlocked door; you can walk right in. A closed mind is like trying to open a bank vault without the combination.

KEY PHRASE

To accomplish this, we will now use what we call a "key phrase." A key phrase is a combination of words that immediately opens the customer's mind and makes him receptive.

Look the customer straight in the eye and say in a firm and authoritative voice, "Mr. Customer, I know one thing: if I'm going to sell you this product or service, I've got to give you a good deal and the best of everything else you expect; because if I don't, I cannot sell you this product or service. Simple as that, isn't it?" Deliver this line with all the sincerity you have within you.

It makes no difference what you are selling: car insurance, houses, appliances, cars, trucks, home improvement, storms and screens, garages, driveways. When asking this question, make him give you an answer. He will usually agree with you.

If you are selling an intangible (like life insurance), you then say, "Mr. Customer, if I showed you a program that was so good and had so many benefits and is so inexpensive you couldn't turn it down, you would have to consider it, wouldn't you?" Again, deliver this line with sincerity.

In every instance, where you use a key phrase, make the customer answer you.

A key phrase must say, in effect, "Mr. Customer, I know in considering my product or service, you want all the best features and benefits that I can possibly give you at the lowest possible price. Mr. Customer, if I cannot give you all of these things, I cannot possibly hope to sell you."

This understanding of the customer's thought and desires not only opens his mind and makes him receptive, but also makes the customer like and respect you, because the customer thinks to himself, "Here is a salesman who is thoughtful and fair. This salesman is making my decision whether to buy or not to buy very easy and uncomplicated. This salesman is not trying to give me a lot of fast talk. He simply says to me, 'Mr. Customer, I know that if I'm going to deal with you, I must give you the very best deal that you can get anywhere at the lowest possible price. And also, my benefits and advantages must match or surpass those found anywhere for less money.' If I feel I am not getting the very best of everything, I simply, without any twinge of conscience, don't have to buy."

The customer will feel that any salesman who is this thoughtful and fair has earned the right to be liked and earned a measure of respect.

Again, I remind you, your delivery is always in a firm and authoritative voice. If you cannot incorporate one of the key phrases I have given you into your sales presentation, then think of a key phrase that would be effective for your particular business. A key phrase must tell your customer you understand that you must either give him everything he could want and desire at the best possible price, or you forfeit the sale.

WE WILL NOW LEARN HOW TO MAKE THE CUSTOMER THINK AND FEEL AS HE DOES. To do this, we will use what we call "Empathy Image." Empathy Image is the ability to make another person think that you think and feel as he does. The more you make the customer feel this, the stronger your control will become. This is important, for it will help you increase your control as you go along.

Empathy Image is accomplished by making statements that make the customer think you have his best interest at heart. These statements should be self-evident truths that are generally on every customer's mind.

For example, you could say, "Mr. Customer, I know that money is not easy to come by, so saving a dollar is always welcome, isn't it?" Or, "Mr. Customer, with today's high prices, I know you want as much value for your dollar as possible, isn't that right?" Or, "Mr. Customer, I know that you have other bills and responsibilities, and money only goes so far; so I'll make sure this product or service is reasonable and fits into your budget, because that's what you're looking for, isn't it?" Always end your statement with a question; because whatever you say, you must get the customer's reaction.

When you finish this paragraph, try to think of statements that can build your Empathy Image. The statement must say, in effect, "Mr. Customer, I want you to know I will do whatever it takes to make this product or service as reasonable and as satisfactory as possible for you." Remember, in building your Empathy Image, always end your statement with a question.

Also, you must never contradict yourself, because once you give the customer cause for doubt, everything is lost.

This course is set up so that all the steps are as mistakeproof as possible. Each step is constructed specifically to draw the customer further under your control. So follow the steps you learn as closely as possible. Mistakes are deadly; don't make the first one.

Now WE SHALL LEARN HOW TO PHRASE YOUR SALES PRESENTATION TO MAKE IT SO EFFECTIVE, THE SALE IS ALMOST AUTOMATIC. In phrasing your sales presentation about your product or service, you never make statements without asking a question, unless giving a command, answering an objection, or giving the customer statistical or pertinent information about your product or service.

The purpose of statistical or pertinent information should be to impress the customer with a product's or service's durability, performance, model, advantages,comfort, beauty, convenience, safety, benefits, price, payments, interest, etc.

After you make a statement to the customer about any of the above (and this is done while looking the customer straight in the eye and in a firm and authoritative voice that rings with authenticity and finality), follow immediately with a question to the customer about the statement you have just made.

For example, you make a statement to the customer about the reasonable price of an item. You follow up immediately with a question that could sound like this: "Mr. Customer, you must admit, with all the features you are getting, the price seems very reasonable, doesn't it?"

Always get an answer to your question, even if you have to repeat the question.

When you just keep making statement after statement to a customer, you don't know one iota of what the customer is thinking. But, coming back with a question, after a statement, you will know exactly what the customer is thinking every minute. This will also aid you in picking the exact minute to close with pinpoint accuracy. When your sales presentation is constructed in this manner, statements followed by questions, you always get the customer's reaction.

Keep your sales presentation as brief as possible while getting the necessary information from the customer which you will need for your close. The less time it takes with a customer, the less chance a customer has to think for himself and get confused. When you perfect this control method of selling, don't be surprised to discover you are selling customers in one-half or one-third the time it took you at first. This method simply gives you the time and means of selling more customers.

I will impress upon you once again something I cannot impress upon you too often or too strenuously: every one of these procedures you are learning must be spoken in a firm and authoritative voice and executed as flawlessly as possible.

While you read and review the steps of this course, write down statements along with corresponding questions about statistical or pertinent information about your particular product or service.

In going through your sales presentation, here is an important point to keep in mind when there is a choice to be made between two or more products, or two or more types of service handled by a company: if the customer wavers between a choice more than an instant too long, step up and make the choice for him immediately. Failure to do so could brake your momentum or stop you in your tracks.

If you control the customer as you should, the customer will accept your advice. To show indecision at such a point would only invite confusion on the part of the customer, and perhaps result in a lost customer.

Now we will learn how to answer objections in one sentence. In answering objections, being brief is a must. Objections or questions about the quality, value, safety, durability, convenience, price, terms, interest, etc., will almost always be raised. There are many reasons a customer will raise objections. One could be that he does not completely believe what you are telling him. Another could be that someone else has told him something different. Another could be that he's trying to make you aware that he has a mind, too, and is not a dummy who doesn't know anything. Or he might be just plain argumentative, which is just his basic character. A person like this will argue with anybody, about anything, just for the sake of argument.

When one asks questions or raises objections about basic features or price, there is almost always genuine concern (whether an item is safe, or durable, or money-saving, or convenient, etc.). In answering, always use reassuring phrases, which instill confidence and assert the need not to worry. Here are four examples:

1. "That's no problem at all, Mr. Customer—none whatsoever."

2. "Oh, no, Mr. Customer, you have nothing to worry about—nothing at all."

3. "You are getting the best rate of interest the law allows, Mr. Customer, the absolute best."

4. "Our policies have the best features that you will find anywhere, Mr. Customer, and that's a fact."

Always repeat the ending as if it were the gospel truth. And never forget, when answering objections or questions of concern, always speak in a firm and authoritative voice and look the customer straight in the eye.

THE NEXT STEP WILL BE ASKING QUESTIONS THAT ALWAYS CALL FOR "YES" OR AFFIRMATIVE ANSWERS. Always ask questions that call for "yes" or affirmative answers, because doing so further increases the control, goodwill, and understanding you have created by using the other steps successfully.

Ask the customer questions about the basic features or advantages of a product or service that are self-evident truths. These questions may be raised or asked at any point of your sales presentation.

The reason for keeping a customer saying "yes" is because when he says "no," he must begin to think of negative reasons to substantiate his position. This can lead to confusion, trouble, and a lost customer.

Here are a few examples of affirmative questions:

1. "You must admit, Mr. Customer, this new car handles like a dream, doesn't it?"
2. "Mr. Customer, this beautiful aluminum siding sure eliminates those tedious and messy painting worries, doesn't it?"
3. "This savings program would give a person just about all the security he could ask for, wouldn't you say so, Mr. Customer?"
4. "That plan you like for your kitchen would have a very striking effect, wouldn't it, Mrs. Customer?"

Whenever you ask these questions, make sure the customer gives you an answer.

Now these are just examples. I'm sure you can think of many questions for your particular product or service that call for "yes" or affirmative answers.

You will learn when to close right to the minute. I use the word "close" in reference to getting a signature. As I mentioned earlier, you begin to close the minute you greet the customer and take immediate control.

One of the most troublesome and heartbreaking problems a salesman faces is not knowing when to ask for the order or signature. This problem has ruined more salesmen than any other single factor. It is like a man groping around in the dark, without rhyme, reason, or purpose. This is something 75 percent of the salesmen today don't know how to do with pinpoint accuracy. It is usually a hit-and-miss proposition, which indicates the salesman is unsuccessful more times than he is successful. Many salesmen ask for the order or signature too soon or too late—losing everything.

I'm going to give you an automatic and systematic way of knowing when to close. You have already learned the following procedures:

1. You took control the minute you greeted the customer.
2. You immediately began to give the customer commands.
3. You used a key phrase, which opened the customer's mind and made him receptive.
4. You showed thoughtfulness and fairness, which made the customer like and respect you.
5. You expressed your Empathy Image, which showed understanding of the customer's side and his problems and made the cus-

tomer think that you think and feel as
he does.

6. In phrasing your sales presentation the way
   you've been taught, you zeroed in on the
   customer's mind and knew exactly what he
   was thinking.

7. When the customer asked questions or
   raised objections, you handled them very
   quickly, with phrases that instilled confidence and assured the customer not to
   worry. This prevents the customer from
   going off on a tangent or getting involved
   in a disagreement that can cause doubt
   and negative thoughts.

8. You always asked questions that called for
   "yes" or affirmative answers, which blanked
   out a negative trend of thought.

We now come to the words "key statistics."
Key statistics truly let you know when to close, right
to the minute. What are key statistics? They are the
features about a product or service upon which you
base your sales presentation.

There are key statistics for every product or
service sold. Examples of key statistics could be the
performance, the model, the convenience, the safety,
the benefits, the advantages, the comfort, the durability, the beauty, the price, the payments, the

interest, etc. These are just a few. I am sure you know what the key statistics connected with your particular product or service are.

When you have affirmative or satisfactory answers for questions about key statistics for your product or service, you are ready to close. Your sales presentation should contain questions about the key statistics of your particular product or service.

Phrase your questions about key statistics so they call for affirmative answers. When you have accomplished this, you immediately prepare your customer for the close.

When you have finished reading this chapter, make up a list of key statistics for your product or service.

THE NEXT STEP IS ASKING FOR THE ORDER OR SIGNATURE. If you have completed all nine previous steps successfully, you will be ready to ask for the order or signature on whatever product or service you are selling.

If you have to write the sales agreement or contract yourself, take out whatever forms or papers you are going to fill in. Before you begin to write, say to the customer in a firm and authoritative voice, "Mr. Customer, I'm just going to show you how this will look." Immediately begin to write. Do not stop writing until you are finished. If the sales agreement is already filled in, merely present it with the words, "Mr. Customer, I want you to see just how this looks."

You must feel that you are in control and you are going to sell, and feel that you are controlling the customer and he is going to buy. You are ready to get the customer's signature. IMPORTANT: Never ask a customer to sign. I repeat: never ask a customer to sign. You command, "Mr. Customer, just put your name right here and I will get this taken care of for you." Point to the spot or X with the pen. Then put the pen where the customer can reach it easily, and look away. Do not watch the customer sign. Do not speak unless he hesitates for one full minute or asks a question.

After the customer signs, explain whatever your type of business necessitates. Then get up immediately and bid the customer good-bye in the same manner as your original greeting, with a firm handshake and a smile, looking him straight in the eye. Your voice is as firm and authoritative at the end as it was at the beginning.

After every sale, tell yourself you are one of the best salesmen in the country and believe you will control every customer completely from beginning to end. Repeat this statement to yourself eight to ten times and say it with power, conviction, and meaning. As a man believes, so he is. You must believe wholeheartedly, with the methods and procedures you are learning today, that you will sell every customer you talk to.

How do you handle problems arising in the final step? That was a job well done. But what if the customer did not sign?

Let us say you've executed all the other steps of this sales training course properly and with finesse. You asked for the order just the way you have learned to do. You waited a full minute, but the customer did not sign. In that minute, the customer has not indicated to you why he has not signed the order or contract.

Point at the X for a signature and again state in a firm tone of voice, "Just put your name there, Mr. Customer, and I'll get this taken care of for you."

You then remain silent and look away again. In most cases, by this time, the customer will say something to the effect that he'd better think it over, or "I'd better go home and talk to my wife," or, if the wife is present, "My wife and I will go home and talk it over," or, "It's too much money," or, "I can't afford it."

Now, if the customer had signed the first time you asked, this information would not be necessary. But if he did not sign, you are at the most crucial point of your sale and you need every bit of ammunition you can muster for the final breakthrough. If not, all is lost.

You could have been flawless throughout the sale, but until you've gotten the customer to take the final step, all else has been in vain.

Now, let's examine the circumstances surrounding a situation in which the customer would not sign the first time you asked him, even though he has been handled properly. We find, in many cases, the customer is not a buyer. To be more dramatic, if you cut the price in half (which you could not economically do), or stretched out the terms of payment twice the legal limit, he still would not buy. He simply is not a buyer.

Now, in some cases, the customer is raising a legitimate objection. When a customer states, "I want to go home and talk to my wife," it's just like that in many families. The husband does not make any decisions to spend money without his wife's consent, and vice versa. It is what is known as "togetherness."

Now your job is to overcome this problem without having the customer break this unwritten, but nevertheless sacred, law between the customer and his wife.

You say, "Mr. Customer, I can understand your not making a decision to spend money without your wife, because I'll be honest—it's something I don't do either."

You then say, "Your wife is probably at home, isn't she?" If he says yes, say, "You know, I usually call my wife or have the salesman do it. Tell you what . . . Mr. Customer, I'll give her a call . . . just to give her an idea of what we're talking about, and then we can go from there."

Try to call the customer's wife yourself. If the customer calls his wife, make sure you talk to the wife first . . . to explain and sell her. Do not let the husband talk until you have done so.

If both husband and wife are there, either in your office or in their home, and their objection is "We want to talk it over," or "We don't think we can afford it," your reply is, "Mr. and Mrs. Customer, you know the reason a person gets up and works every day is to get some of the things out of life that he wants. But if you don't, what's the use of working? You might as well stay home all day and have nothing. It's only money, and you can't take it with you. You know something? Henry Ford was the richest man that ever lived. You know how much he took with him when he died? Not one red cent! So, folks, you might as well enjoy yourselves while you're here. Just put your name right here and I'll get this taken care of for you."

If you are selling an intangible such as life

insurance, you might then say, "Mr. Customer, you will have to spend money that does not seem necessary or does not give you immediate benefits that you can wear, ride in, or show off. Every year you pay out about $2,000 or more in taxes—federal, state, sales, excise, etc. You have absolutely no control of how much you have to pay. Today's society demands we pay a great deal of money in taxes whether we want to or not; today's society demands we have adequate insurance to cover our needs. To make this as easy and as comfortable as possible, you tell me how much you can afford, how you want to pay, when you want to pay, and what benefits you would like to receive. Mr. Customer, you must admit with all the benefits, protection, and peace of mind you will have, the amount is very small, isn't it? Just put your name right here and I will get this program started for you."

In conclusion, I state that when an objection is raised in the final step of signing the order or contract, and you have taken control of the customer using the method and procedures you have learned, increasing your control as you went along, if the customer then makes no conscious effort to buy the product or service you are selling, I then conclude he is not a buyer at this particular time, and will call him later. I'll keep his name for future reference.

4

What Are Some of the Other Sales Methods, and Why Don't They Work on Today's Buyer?

Before beginning to discuss other sales methods, let's list them first:

1. The "hard" sell
2. The "soft" sell
3. The "negative" sell
4. The "beggar's" sell
5. The "always smiling" sell
6. The "I'll give them my serious look" sell
7. The "I know it all" sell
8. The "scared to death" sell
9. The "look good, no talk" sell
10. The "I don't give a damn" sell
11. The "I hope I get lucky today" sell
12. The "I'm gonna love you to death" sell
13. The "I can't understand" sell

You have probably heard the saying, "Time changes all things." That statement was true in the beginning of time, and shall be true in the end. What was apropos yesterday is not apropos today. What was charming or chic twenty years ago is not charming or chic today. The art of power and control selling feels the very same way about sales. We must be able to adapt to cope with today's modern buyer, or become ineffective or unproductive.

We will explore almost all the different sales methods. We will analyze them one by one to see why they don't work effectively anymore. We will cover some that have never worked effectively. Let's start with the three most popular: the "hard" sell, the "soft" sell, and the "negative" sell.

THE "HARD" SELL

Bob is a disciple of the "hard" sell. He thinks it's the only way to go. His motto is, once you put the pressure on the customer, keep the pressure on until the customer caves in completely or runs out the door; or, if you are selling to him in his home, keep the pressure on until the customer asks you to leave in a polite (or not so polite) way. Bob believes in sales it's now or never.

Bob is a very pleasant fellow when he engages

in everyday conversation. But when it comes to using intimidation to sell, Bob is in his glory. Bob greets his customers warmly. He discusses his particular product or service with his customer in the same manner. He still appears to be a pleasant salesman to the customer. When Bob has completed his sales presentation for his customers, he fills out the order or contract for his particular business. At this point, he tells the customer to sign the document. The customer says he will not sign at this time for whatever reason (and there are many). Bob says, "Come on Mr. Jones, sign here and we'll get this fixed up for you." The customer refuses again: the situation turns into a battle of wills. Bob asks the customer to sign again, and again, and again, and again. He does not take "no" for an answer. Bob is determined to keep the pressure on until the customer either makes or breaks. In most cases, the customer feels so uncomfortable in such a pressured situation that he will either leave Bob's place of business or, if Bob is on the customer's premises, he will somehow get Bob to leave. The customer will also avoid Bob in the future. The pressure Bob exerts turns the customer off. The "hard" sell has had its day. Today's customer is too confused, has too many options, and is too mobile to sit still for that kind of pressure.

THE "SOFT" SELL

When you see John doing his thing, the "soft" sell, it's hard to tell who is the salesman and who is the customer. If both John and the customer were behind partitions and you could not see them, you would think they were a couple of old friends who had not seen each other for a while. You hear them talking about their kids' little league baseball or football, going fishing and "the big one that got away," where they went on their vacations and what they did, what the wife did last week and what she plans to do next week, the illnesses the kids had last year, the aching back, the rheumatism in the knee. It's usually the customer who will direct the conversation back toward the business, by asking some questions about the product or service. John seems as though he would enjoy talking about everything but business. Even when John talks about business, he still comes across like a neighbor talking over the fence about some minor neighborhood event. If the customer tells John he would like to purchase whatever product or service John has to offer, John will lackadaisically get together whatever papers he needs; he will then suggest that if the customer would like to complete things now, fine; if not, some later date would be fine, too. Whatever the customer says would be fine. John's motto seems to be, never push the customer; let the customer sell himself.

Just as the two words "hard" and "soft" are complete opposites, the two methods of selling are as different as night and day; one is as ineffective as the other for today's modern customer. There must be a line between professional selling and just rapping with your neighbor across the fence. There must be some power and control directed from the salesman to the customer. One of the keys to successful selling is being able to use power and control to think for the customer rather than let the customer think and act for himself.

THE "NEGATIVE" SELL

Tom is a believer in the "negative" sell. Tom himself is a negative person. One of Tom's favorite phrases is, "They're not buyers, they're just lookers." One of his favorite words is *can't*; "they can't do this," or "they can't do that." Tom limits himself consciously and unconsciously by the way he thinks.

I'm sure you have heard of the term "bait and switch." This term comes from advertising an item or service at a very low price. When the customer comes in to buy, he is told the advertised item is so cheaply made and so unreliable, it is not worth having, or that the cheapest service is so ineffective it is not worth buying. Tom's negative sell philosophy is just the reverse. When going through his sales pitch with a customer, if a buyer admits liking the best and most expensive product or service you have to offer, Tom will try to sell the customer the less expensive product or service. Tom's strategy is to put the customer down a bit with statements such as, "Only the well-to-do can afford the most expensive product or service," or "Only the most urbane or discriminating person will settle for nothing but the best."

Once Tom has laid the ground rules for this game, it's up to the customers to prove they deserve the best and are willing to pay for it. They must prove they belong to the select few, the urbane and discriminating buyers Tom has spoken of. Tom keeps showing these customers the least expensive item or service until the customers demand to be shown the best.

If the customer doesn't buy anything, Tom indicates in so many words that maybe the customer can't even afford his cheapest product or service, hoping the customer will take the "I'll show him attitude" and buy something just to prove Tom wrong—make him eat his own words, so to speak.

The problem with this method of selling is that

most customers walk out or are turned off prematurely because they don't like to be put down or made to feel small. Today's modern customers are not that egotistical. Keeping up with the Joneses and showing status symbols are not that important anymore. Rampant inflation and a declining standard of living are making all of us more thrifty than ever before. Tom is employing a psychological trick that even in its heyday was a gamble, at best. With *The Art of Power and Control Selling*, you don't have to gamble anymore.

THE "BEGGAR'S" SELL

Walt has been in sales for ten years. Without the proper training, meaning *The Art of Power and Control Selling*, Walt has had a very tough time making ends meet, taking care of his wife and five kids. Walt believes in big families because large families are a part of his family's history—"A bunch of kids and a flock of grandchildren," as Walt's father would brag. Walt's father always said, "Big families are happier families." That may have been true before double-digit inflation. I don't know about the happier part, but I do know they're a lot poorer. Big families are getting to be less popular with each passing year. What has all this got to do

with the "beggar's" sell? Well, Walt kind of slipped
into this kind of selling by accident and has been
doing it ever since.

With prices rising at such a rapid rate, Walt
found it harder and harder to provide the necessities
for his large family. About four years ago, Walt was
having his average year, which was not too good in
the best of times when inflation rates were much
lower. Walt found the going tough. His wife was
pregnant with their fifth child. Walt's finances were
as tight as a fat lady's girdle. Walt was in his office
trying to close a difficult buyer and not getting anywhere. He needed this deal in the worst way. His
family's finances were between a rock and a hard
place. Walt looked at the picture of his family he
kept on his desk and realized he had not made
enough money to buy groceries. Walt looked the
customer straight in the eye, with a pained and
hopeless expression, and pleaded, "If you don't buy,
my family will have to go hungry. Please don't let
that happen." The customer looked at Walt's expression and the picture of Walt's family, and
decided to buy. From that day on, when no other
means would work, Walt would *beg* his customers
to buy, because his family would go hungry if they
didn't buy. Walt even went so far to take a large
separate picture of his spastic son in a wheelchair.
This became the pattern of his sales procedure, to

beg because his wife or kids were sick and talk about the backbreaking doctor bills for his spastic son. The statement that his family would not eat unless the customer bought was one of his favorites.

This approach got Walt a lot of sympathy and a few sales. It got to the point that Walt became hooked on sympathy, getting people to feel sorry for him, and this began to be as important as getting the sale. Walt began to feel sorry for himself. Walt was now dealing from a position of pure weakness rather than strength, which by its own nature is self-defeating. Walt is still begging, but without much success. What Walt really needs is *The Art of Power and Control Selling*. He will never have to beg again.

THE "ALWAYS SMILING" SELL

You'd better have good teeth for this one. If a dentist had a clientele of this kind of salespeople, he'd be a rich man. Dave was a smiler; to him smiling was selling, and selling was smiling. Dave had been in sales for five years, and he had been constantly smiling for five years. Dave had even practiced smiling into the mirror for long periods of time. He wanted to have the perfect smile. Dave's dentist played an important part in his life.

I must admit, it may not have been a perfect smile, but it wasn't far from it. Dave's father had called him a natural-born salesman. I contend that salesmen are made, not born.

Dave was a nice-looking guy and he had a dazzling smile. He would turn on his smile the minute he greeted the customer. The smile would be on during the entire sales presentation. It is impossible to get a serious point across or make yourself sound serious unless you look serious. Dave believed if he made himself look happy, other people would be happy to be around him and deal with him. Dave believed it is harder to say "no" to a salesman with a big smile than to a salesman who appears to be serious or sour. Dave would use phrases like, "Isn't that nice?" (Smile) "I know that protection would be worth having." (Smile) "Can we get this set up for you?" (Smile). Smile, smile, and smile some more.

Dave reminds me of that beautiful girl who was always primping and pampering the outer self but neglecting the inner self. I'm sure we have all heard the saying, "Beauty and no brains." Dave's problem is that he has taken only one attribute, his smile, from the many attributes a successful salesperson should try to develop. Dave is trying to base his sale success on just two things, his smile and likability. With such limited tools, Dave may win a sales battle here and there, but he most surely will lose the war.

Smiles are appropriate at the proper time and in the right context, but there must also be strength, power, and control for successful selling.

THE "I'LL GIVE THEM MY SERIOUS LOOK" SELL

We have just discussed Dave, who smiles all of the time. Now, we are going to meet his complete opposite—Ray, who hardly ever smiles at all. Ray believes that making a living is a very serious business and is not really something to smile about. Ray thinks by looking serious, he will convey to the customer that he is a no-nonsense salesman who takes his business the same way.

When a salesperson greets a customer, you customarily expect the salesperson to smile or return the customer's smile. A smile usually designates friendliness or a feeling of goodwill toward another person. Not smiling at all usually appears to be just the opposite. Ray is from the school that believes that smiling a great deal means you're easy and the customer might take advantage of you. Ray believes that by only showing his serious side, he encourages the customer to stick strictly to the business at hand

and not get too close in a personal way. Ray and salespeople who think like him, if put under closer psychological examination, would probably tend to be loners who keep everybody at arm's length until they feel they know others well enough to feel comfortable. This kind of reaction is not conducive to good personal relations of any kind, and especially not in sales.

The Art of Power and Control Selling will teach Ray to rise above his basic personality. By learning what to say and how to say it and by following the many other valuable directions in this book, Ray will be on the way to becoming the success he would like to be.

THE "I KNOW IT ALL" SELL

I am sure that most of us know this kind of person, whether he may be a fellow salesperson, an acquaintance, or a friend. This kind of person is offensive in a sales situation, and just as offensive in a non-sales situation. Any person who acts and talks as if he knows it all can easily be grating on the nerves and the ears. Ron's philosophy is, "the more you know, the more successful you will be," which is a fair and true assessment when taken in context. But some of Ron's reasoning got twisted around somehow. Ron reasoned, if he knew a lot and was not afraid to show it, he could be good. Carrying this reasoning even further, if he could show he knew more than most, he would be great. Therefore, if he knew it all and made his customers aware of this fact, Ron could be the GREATEST.

Ron would tell his customers what they should buy, when they should buy, how they should buy, and from whom the item or service should be bought. The "whom" was obviously himself. Ron was a nonlistener, which means when a customer would try to explain what he wanted to buy, Ron would interrupt in mid-sentence to impart his own thoughts. He believed that even when he gave the customer bad information or misinformation, if he appeared to know it all, the customer would not doubt him. Ron would discuss subjects he knew little or nothing about. When customers would hear some of Ron's inaccurate explanations and sometimes gross misinformation, this would degrade Ron's credibility to the extent that his customer would not believe Ron in the business he really knew.

The art of power and control selling believes in explicit honesty. Always tell the truth. When Ron learns the art of power and control selling, the truth will become one of his greatest assets.

THE "SCARED TO DEATH" SELL

Charles is a good conversationalist, likable, with a winning smile. When in a related environment away from business, you could not meet a person with a more pleasant personality—but when it comes to approaching a customer for business and attempting to make a sale, Charles becomes scared to death. When I say scared to death, the only thing Charles does not do is die. It is not the startling kind of fright where your heart pounds furiously, your pupils dilate into a wild-eyed look, your whole body tightens up, and you can feel the adrenaline racing through your body. Although Charles has felt some of the above when he is with a customer, his fear is usually the kind of a feeling that numbs his body, takes away his energy, and makes him mentally and physically weak. Charles knows the feeling well.

You must wonder what Charles is afraid of. Is he afraid of not being liked? Is he afraid of not being able to match wits with the customer? Is he afraid that by not making this sale, he will not have enough money to meet his obligations? Charles does not understand why he is afraid. He only knows that he is. Charles gets that numb kind of fear that tightens the throat so his words do not flow in any sort of smooth conversational manner. A feeling of inadequacy sweeps over Charles like a fog. He some-

times cannot look the customer in the eye because
of fear. Even his physical movements become un-
coordinated, and he drops and bumps into things.
Charles cannot deliver a statement with any sort of
power. He has no control whatsoever, which means
the customer can take over completely—for Charles,
another frustrating and scared sales presentation,
resulting in another lost sale.

When Charles learns the art of power and control selling, being scared will be a thing of the past.

THE "LOOK GOOD, NO TALK" SELL

Lennie had a shock of curly black hair, finely
chiseled features, and nice, even white teeth—he
was a former football and basketball player. He kept
himself in shape working out with weights, jogging,
and playing handball. Lennie had the handsome
body to complement his good looks. He knew he
was a good-looking guy, and anyone with 20/20
vision would agree. Lennie loved to take off his suit
jacket to expose his bulging muscles, broad shoulders,
and small waist. He had his clothes tailored to show
off his athletic body in the best way. He knew he
was an attractive man and did nothing to hide the
fact. He was the dream of many females and the
envy of many males.

Lennie got into sales because even without a

college education, he wanted a job where he could dress professionally and have an opportunity to make big money. His high school counselor knew that Lennie was only passed in high school because he was a star football and basketball player. The counselor agreed that Lennie's athletic vigor and good looks would be an asset in the sales profession. Being a sports star, Lennie found everything had been very easy for him. He had girls, an after-school job that paid more than the work required, and a car given to him by proud parents. Lennie lived the good life.

When Lennie got into sales, he didn't believe in learning product knowledge and giving a detailed sales presentation; he would use as little as possible. Lennie believed that if you were handsome, which he was, dressed to a T, which he did, looked like a movie star, and had the body of a Greek god, you were one of God's chosen people. He thought that since he had all those qualities, his customers would automatically like him and buy from him. Lennie reasoned that customers buy from salespeople they like, and besides, don't all the advertising agencies use good looks and sex appeal to sell everything from soup to nuts on TV, newspapers, etc.? Well, Lennie didn't have much success in sales. He always had many females coming by to see him. He sold to a few and made love to many.

After a few years in the business without much success, Lennie learned the "look good, don't talk" method does not work. It may get you a lot of attention from the opposite sex, but it won't make you a success. Lennie decided he wanted to become one of the best in his business. We're just glad *The Art of Power and Control Selling* is here to help Lennie achieve his goal.

THE "I DON'T GIVE A DAMN" SELL

If you've ever met a guy who had a perennial chip on his shoulder, you're going to recognize Roger. Roger's two favorite expressions are, "Tell him he can go stick it in his ear" (whatever that means) and "I don't give a damn." Roger has been in sales for eleven years, and he makes an average income for salespeople in his business. But with the double-digit inflation we face today, "average" does not cut the mustard anymore. Roger's wife works for one of the airlines and makes a good salary, without which Roger's family could not make ends meet. Roger's "I don't give a damn" sales approach surfaces when he meets tough sales resistance, or when a customer gives a reason for not buying that Roger doesn't like.

To say that Roger's "I don't give a damn" sales approach surfaces quite often would be an understatement, since trying to sell today's buyer is tougher than ever before. That chip on Roger's shoulder is constantly falling off. He argues with the customers, tells them they don't know what they are talking about, and makes statements such as, "Mr. or Mrs. Customer, if you know so much about my business, you should be sitting in my chair. Mr. Customer, I wouldn't tell you how to do your job, I'm certainly not going to let you tell me how to do mine." Roger's favorite descriptions for people who don't buy are "idiots" or "flakes." What Roger doesn't realize is that his attitude and his lack of power and control are his downfall.

When Roger learns the art of power and control selling, he will finally have the tools to change him from an average salesman with a chip on his shoulder to an outstanding salesman who sells with confidence and effectiveness, and has money in the bank.

I am sure there are a lot more of you like Roger out there. When a sale is not going your way, your only weapon is to get angry and verbally berate the customer, and speak of him in derogatory terms when he is gone. The art of power and control selling will do away with this attitude forever.

THE "I HOPE I GET LUCKY TODAY" SELL

Doris had been in sales for three years. Doris had a B.A. degree in education. Not being able to find a job in the already overcrowded teaching field, she took a job in sales. Women are becoming more prevalent in sales every day, just as women are entering other fields once dominated by men. Women are taking sales positions that were previously held by men. Believe it or not, some sales jobs were the last bastions of male chauvinism. Just think about that for a minute. We have had women physicians, attorneys, and educators for years. We even had women pilots fifty years ago. But women have just begun to enter sales in numbers the last ten to fifteen years. Just as with a male, a female must be qualified to get the job done.

Doris overheard her male counterparts say that selling was 90 percent luck. No matter how hard you worked, it made no difference; you just had to be lucky. "I hope I get lucky today" became Doris's favorite saying. Doris had let the attitude that good luck made you successful and bad luck did just the opposite become her whole way of thinking. Nothing could be further from the truth. Working hard, having the proper tools, and working smart are the keys to successful selling. I think you would be surprised at the number of people in sales who really believe beyond a shadow of a doubt that luck does play an important part in their sales success. This is not true now, and never has been. I think a great many of us grow up believing that luck will play a major role in our personal as well as our business lives. Lady Luck, to many, has become a mysterious princess who can reach out and change one's entire life. I believe after careful scrutiny and looking at the people who you have called "lucky" for having attained success, if you were to question these people at length, you would find real qualities such as desire, perseverance, and working hard and smart to be the foundation upon which their success is built.

So leave luck to the gamblers. Build a solid foundation with *The Art of Power and Control Selling,* and people will say you are lucky, too.

THE "I'M GONNA LOVE YOU TO DEATH" SELL

Rose was in her second year in sales. She thought it was such an exciting way to make a living. She got to travel around, stay in the best hotels, and meet new and interesting people. Rose was a gregarious young woman with a dazzling smile and a beautiful figure. Rose came from a broken home; her father had deserted her mother and five kids. Her mother died two years later. Rose was raised by her grandmother, who was a strict and stern disciplinarian and did not understand the younger generation. Rose grew up without the parental love that is needed to give a child a well-adjusted start in life, especially during the adolescent years when young adults are trying to sort out some of life's problems.

Rose was a brilliant student, which enabled her to get a college scholarship. In high school, Rose had gotten intimately involved with one of her teachers who projected a father image. Rose majored in marketing. She took a job in sales when she graduated. Rose was beginning her third year in sales and was not satisfying herself or her superiors with her progress. If her superiors had known the methods she was using, they would have known why.

Being an attractive young lady, Rose had always been a charmer. She had always used her charms to her advantage with males. When Rose first took this job, she found that all of her customers were males. She thought to herself, "This job is going to be a snap." When Rose would make an initial contact, she would dress very seductively. Rose enjoyed receiving male attention and affection and enjoyed returning the same.

A psychiatrist would probably say her love-starved childhood and adolescence played a big part in her actions. Not many customers could resist Rose's charms. Using these charms got Rose a tremendous amount of attention and affection, which often turned intimate. There's an old adage that business and pleasure don't mix. Rose was to learn this lesson the hard way.

Had Rose stuck strictly to business and not depended on her good looks and charms, she could have succeeded even beyond her fondest hopes. Her almost genius IQ plus her strong desire to succeed and her likeable personality could have made her a winner. By being overly charming and seductive, using sex appeal and even sex to get business, Rose was breaking every sound business principle in the books. In other words, Rose was using charm and sex in a roundabout way to get business, which she would turn into cash as commission for sales. Rose could have just as well taken the direct route to the money by proclaiming she was a hooker—which, in reality, she was. It was a known fact among her customers that sex with Rose could be had by placing a small order for something they needed anyway. Not only didn't her methods work, the guilt complex and mental strain almost caused a nervous breakdown. When Rose learns that power and control and not sex will get the job done, she will be able to harness her natural talents and become one of the premier salespeople in her field.

THE "I CAN'T UNDERSTAND" SELL

Ron has been in sales for six years and he can't understand why he has not accomplished more than he has. Ron cannot understand why he has not been promoted when people who have been with the company less time have been. Ron can't understand when he works so hard and puts in long hours and doesn't make more money.

When Ron is through making his sales presentation, which is well prepared, and he gets down to the bottom line and asks the buyer for the order or his signature, the buyer often replies, "I'm not going to sign now, I'm going to think about this for a few days," or "I've got to check with my wife," or "I'm going to wait and see how the economy is going before I make a decision." Ron's all-time favorite replies are, "Mr. Buyer, this is the perfect time to buy, and I can't understand why you feel this way," or "Mr. Buyer, this policy gives you just the protection you and your family need. I can't understand why you won't take it," or "Mr. Buyer, I just can't for the life of me understand how you can turn down such a heck of a deal."

You know, the tragic thing about the whole situation is, Ron really *does not* understand why customers will say no after a sales presentation that is well planned and well executed. Ron's inability to understand stems from the fact that he does not have at his disposal the most modern and effective weapons to cope with today's modern buyer. When Ron says he doesn't understand, that's just another way of saying he cannot handle today's modern buyer, who is so confused about so many different things, events, and crises.

When Ron learns the art of power and control selling, he will be able to skillfully lead the buyers out of the darkness of confusion into the light of his power and control, and lead them as if he had a magic wand controlling their thoughts and actions.

5

The Pressure of Draw or Commission Sales and How to Adapt

A commission sales career is probably the toughest way to make a living ever devised by man. I am making no reference to the physical work involved, because that is almost nil. I am referring to the unrelenting mental pressure that a salesperson who is on a commission or draw basis must face every day, day in, day out, week in, week out, month in, month out, year after year after year. It's the pressure that can break up marriages or bend them beyond repair. It's the pressure that can sow the seeds of discontent between the salesman and his wife or his sons and daughters. It's the pressure that can change or alter a salesperson's personality for the worse. It's the pressure that can make you so mentally exhausted that sleeping fifteen hours at a time will not cause you to feel rested. I know you have often wondered what you can do to get relief from the pressure.

We all know that a certain amount of pressure or stress is healthy and productive. But in cases where pressure has been extremely severe for long periods of time, the effect can be devastating, mentally and physically.

Salespeople working on a commission or draw face other problems that are part of our business. They may have a feeling of being weak and helpless, unable to affect their own destinies. Thousands and thousands of salespeople drift along with the tide living with fear; fear that they will not be able to get their jobs done effectively and profitably; fear that their next customer will not respond to them or be convinced by their sales presentation; fear that they are not true professionals in their business and may never be; fear that they are not in control of their own future, and not knowing what to do about it, which only compounds that fear. They may fear a lack of control over their customers, their sales situation, or their work habits. They can experience the feeling that they are not effective, competent, and able human beings.

EXAMPLES OF PRESSURES

Al worked as head shipping clerk for a large wholesale plumbing firm for ten years. Al was married, had three kids, a loving wife, a nice home, and was a regular churchgoer. He was active in the Boy Scouts and had risen to the position of Scout Leader. He was an active participant in P.T.A. meetings.

Al was graduated third in his class in high school. He had two years of college when he married his high school sweetheart. She became pregnant five months after their marriage. With a wife and baby on the way, Al could not make ends meet with a part-time job; so Al dropped out of college, hoping he could return at a later date to finish. Al knew without a college degree his money-making potential was not the best. So Al took a full-time job at the plumbing firm where he had been working part-time. The money wasn't great, but it was a living. Al was the all-American boy there—bright, intelligent, and outstanding, with a ready smile and winning ways.

Al had ambitions of going to law school after he had graduated from college and to use all his attributes to become an outstanding attorney. Had Al's dream been realized, he probably would have made a name for himself in the field of law.

Al loved his wife very much and the prospect of becoming a father made him glow. Al accepted this job in the plumbing company's shipping department and silently vowed to himself he would become the best. Using the same personal qualities that he had in abundance, in eighteen months Al got a promotion and a nice raise. Another promotion and another raise followed, but while this was happening there was another baby, a mortgage on a house, and car payments.

In the fifth year a third baby came, and Al gave up all hopes of college and law school after six years with the company. Al was promoted to head of the shipping department. The job carried a title, but not much money. Al knew he did not want to get stuck in that job for the rest of his life.

As the next few years rolled by, Al knew in his heart he was worth a lot more money than he was making. Believing he could not go back to college because of family responsibilities—a wife whom he loved very much and kids he simply adored—he began to think about an occupation that would pay him what he believed he was worth. After looking and analyzing the jobs available to a person without a college degree, he settled on sales. His choice was narrowed down to commission sales and selling directly to the consumer.

He then had to decide what product or service he would like to sell. He had an uncle in California who sold insurance for one of the major companies. Al's uncle drove a new luxury car every year and lived in an expensive home. Al called his uncle to get some of the pros and cons of the insurance business. There was nothing that Al's uncle loved to talk about more than the insurance business. He had been with the same company for twenty-four years. After a long, stimulating sales talk about the insurance business, Al's uncle suggested that Al get a job with his company, which had a branch office in Al's hometown.

The uncle even offered to call and get Al a job interview, which was tantamount to getting the job, with his uncle making the recommendation. Al thanked his uncle profusely and hung up the phone with an air of jubilation.

Al called his wife into the kitchen, and over a cup of coffee he told her of his plans and his conversation with his uncle. He explained for the first six months of his training period, he would be on salary while learning the insurance business. He told his wife his training salary would be more than the salary at the job he presently held. His wife could feel the excitement in his voice and see the sparkle in his eyes—the kind she had not seen in a long, long time. Al's wife began to get excited, too. However, change, even when it is good, is often frightening. Discarding the old habits that she and her husband had become accustomed to, and a job situation that had become so familiar gave Al's wife a very eerie feeling.

Al spoke again, telling how much money his uncle had made the last year. This was five times as much as Al made as a shipping clerk at the plumbing company. His eyes were sparkling more than ever now. His wife hadn't seen that kind of sparkle since before they were married. She remembered seeing the same sparkle when Al told her about going to law school and becoming a lawyer. She remembered the guilt she felt about getting pregnant so soon after their marriage. Then came the first child, the mortgage on their house, another child, and more bills. Each new baby and each new bill were nails in the coffin that contained Al's dreams of going back to college and then to law school. That coffin was buried along with Al's dreams. She could see Al reaching for the resurrection of dreams that had long ago been buried. Al was going to resurrect those dreams and breathe life into them again. If Al could not be an attorney, he was determined to be a success. Not many men or women have a second chance. Al's wife could see the sparkle in his eyes and the determination in his expression. Al was so excited he could hardly sleep that night, knowing his uncle was going to call the very next day to set up an appointment.

Al, too, was frightened of change. He was about to leave the comradeship and familiarity of the only job he had ever known. Some of his closest friends

were fellow employees. The familiar faces and
friendly surroundings were going to be a thing of
the past. He remembered having the same feelings
when he left his home, his parents, brothers, and
sisters to get married. He was about to leave again
and begin a new phase in his life.

When Al informed his plant supervisor about
his intended plans, his supervisor was so shocked
that he couldn't speak for a full minute. His supervisor knew Al had more brains and talent than his
job called for. Al's supervisor also knew that he was
underemployed and underpaid. The supervisor had
word from the top that Al was in the company's
future plans, and the next job up the ladder was
supervisor. But the man holding that job, Al's
supervisor, did not plan on retiring for about ten
years.

Al's supervisor had no choice but to accept Al's
two weeks' notice. When word spread about Al's
leaving, the whole company came by to express to
Al just how much they enjoyed working with him.
Even the owner came by to tell Al how much he
would be missed and wished him the best of luck.
Al hoped they all understood his reasons for leaving.
The last day of work, Al walked around all day with
a lump as big as a plum in his throat. This was
going to be a very sad day in Al's life and a sad day
for many of his co-workers because he was so well

liked. This bright, intelligent, outgoing guy with the winning smile was going to be genuinely missed.

Those last two weeks were two of the hardest in Al's life. Al tried to understand that there are changes and challenges in everyone's life, and this was one of his.

The first days at the new company were "meet-the-other-people-and-get-acquainted" days. Then began a three-week training period in another city hundreds of miles away. Al would fly home on weekends to be with his family. Those three weeks passed quickly. With the cushion of a salary to rely on, Al went about learning the insurance business, and Al's wife was content. Actually, they had more money than before and Al never missed an opportunity to remind his wife of this fact.

After the third month, Al's wife noticed he seemed more tense than she had ever seen him before. Al's reason was that he was more intense about this job. He repeated, "It's only natural the tension would be greater." Going into the sixth month, Al knew the cushion of a salary would be lifted and he would be strictly on commission. Al was not worried—a little apprehensive, maybe—but not worried. Al's district manager and immediate supervisor were impressed with his winning ways. And he was good with people. The first month off salary, Al had a better than average month. Al's wife began to notice that Al spent less time playing with the kids and was not as tolerant with them as he had been in the past. She attributed these changes to the long hours he put in. She also began to notice Al coming home a little intoxicated—not that Al didn't take an occasional drink every now and then, but that was usually at a party, or when they went out for dinner. Al could not put his finger on his problem at the time. He was beginning to show the first symptoms of pressure—pressure that comes because a salesman is not able to control the people he is selling. The salesman himself was being controlled.

Al began to feel his wife did not understand the nature of his job—the frustration, the aggravation, the long hours, the tension he had to put up with to make a living in draw or commission sales. They began to argue and disagree about small and insignificant things. Al became less tolerant of the kids.

The months turned into years. Al began to drink more and more. He began to stay out later and later. The next step was an affair with a woman who, he thought, understood him and did not nag. Al had no more time for the Boy Scouts. He sent his wife to the P.T.A. meetings. After five years of that kind of life, Al's wife filed for divorce. She blamed him for his drinking, for his affairs, and for not being the kind of family man she thought she had married. He blamed her for not being understanding and for being insensitive to the problems and pressures that any salesperson selling on a draw or commission must face.

I must confess, this is a fictitious story. Al is not a person I have known. He is a combination of people I have known in my twenty-five years in sales. Most of you who are in sales started out working on an hourly or salary basis. You changed jobs because you felt you weren't making enough money, or weren't making as much money as you felt you were worth. You wanted a job with more prestige or one that seemed more professional. Many of you were married before you got involved in sales. Many of you have gotten divorced since you've been in sales.

Pressure and fear can change your whole personality. Some of you who never drank alcoholic beverages before have started drinking. Some of you who were drinking moderately are drinking a lot more. And there are some of you who are on the verge of becoming alcoholics. It's the pressure of having a job where you have to prove yourself every day, every week, every month, and every year. In sales where you work strictly on a draw or commission, you are only as good as your last week's or last month's paycheck. With some occupations, your past reputation will carry you through and keep you on the job, even though your most productive days are behind you. In other occupations, even though your competence and skills are not up to par and your abilities are questionable, you keep your well-paying job because you have seniority. With some union jobs, it is all but impossible to have an incompetent employee fired.

With people in sales, it seems that you are tempting the fickle finger of fate every day. Your sales performance is there for all the world to see. It's like a neon sign. It's shown in how much you have made and how much you have sold if you are inept, or incompetent, or unproductive. You can bet there won't be a union around to take your case to the Supreme Court when you are fired for one of the above reasons. The only whimper of protest you hear will be your own. It is you against the world. And you damn well better have the best weapons possible to fight the momentous battle in which you find yourself engaged. I mean the battle to make enough money to adequately take care of yourself and your family, and to overcome the pressure of being in sales. And it's not enough just being able to cope; you must be able to cope magnificently and eliminate your fear of not being able to handle the job. *The Art of Power and Control Selling* promises to eliminate the pressure.

We will eliminate the pressure by giving you more confidence in your ability than ever before. We will eliminate the pressure by giving you more effectiveness as a salesman than you've ever had before. We will eliminate the pressure by giving you more respect for yourself as a dynamic, productive human being than you've ever had before. We will eliminate the pressure by giving you assurance when you meet the customer in the arena of sales. Winning will become a part of your life.

6

How to Really Become a True Professional in Your Business

Now that you have come this far, your accumulation of knowledge has grown. Each chapter is written in a specific order for a very specific reason. We have staged each chapter to show all the parts in relation to the whole of this new and dynamic method of combining power and control for successful selling beyond your wildest dreams. All of the lessons learned in the previous chapters are parts of the whole that will help you to really become a true professional in your business.

There are specifics you will be given to think about in relation to your type of sales, your company, etc. These specifics will assist you in really becoming a true professional in your business. These specifics are:

1. Understanding the environment in which you can be most effective.

2. Understanding the environment in which you will perform best.
3. Understanding the products or services that are best suited to your particular talents.
4. Is your company's method of doing business best for you?
5. Do the personalities of the people you work with and for (including other salespeople, sales manager, district manager, etc.) help you to be the best you can be?
6. What is the chemistry in your company in reference to your "business health" and business happiness?

Before we tackle the business of how to really become a true professional in your business, let's review the previous chapters to understand how the parts work in relation to the whole. The "whole" is to become one of the best salesmen in your business through the art of power and control selling.

Each chapter is structured to give you a step-by-step approach to provide you with all the weapons you will need to make the art of power and control selling the key—the key to open the doors of success you have dreamed about. Each chapter is as important as the others. Strive to learn each lesson well to reach your goal and become the best in your business.

Chapter 1 stated that confusion is the salesperson's mortal enemy. I will make this statement again as emphatically as I can. Once a customer becomes confused, you have struck out. Customers who are confused cannot and will not make a decision. The art of power and control selling eliminates confusion as a problem in constructing your sale. If anyone would ask me to use one word to describe the most serious and damaging barrier to a successful sale, that one word would be *confusion*. Remember, confusion can kill more sales than any other single factor.

Chapter 2 concentrated on making yourself mentally tough. You must become mentally tough to make the art of power and control selling work the miracles I have promised. In the art of power and control selling, you are dealing from a position of power and strength. I have spoken of developing a will that can smash down a brick wall and break through a steel door. I believe if this mental energy could be transferred into physical energy, it could literally break down the bricks, mortar, and steel. There are other advantages to becoming mentally tough. You will find as your success in business improves, your personal life will improve, not because you are making more money, but because personal dealings and situations that were problems before will no longer be problems. Mental toughness will give you the mental stamina you need to wade through these problems with ease. You will find yourself dealing with people and problems from a position of strength rather than from a position of weakness. This newly found power will have a magnetic effect upon others. They will be drawn to you. Mental toughness gives you confidence in yourself and in your ability to get the job done. Mental toughness will give you a self-assurance that others will notice and recognize. It does not matter what position you presently hold in your company, from newly hired salesman all the way up to vice-president in charge of sales or marketing. Your superiors will feel your sense of power and control whenever they are around you.

Because chapter 3 is the title chapter of this book, I'm sure you realize I have attached a special significance to this chapter. Rather than recap at this point, I would like you to reread Chapter 3, again, again, and then some more. Chapter 3 is the tie that binds. When you have mastered the methods and techniques throughout the book, chapter 3 is going to tie this into a neat little package called success.

Chapter 4 discussed other sales methods and why they don't work. I included this chapter in the book because millions of salespeople selling today don't even know, from a psychological standpoint, why their particular method is not working. They just know it's not getting the job done. These sales-people attribute their lack of success to a variety of reasons. Some even border on the absurd. To cite some of the reasons:

1. The customer was just plain dumb.
2. The customer was stupid.
3. The customer's wife was dumb or stupid.
4. They both were idiots.
5. They were full of bull.
6. It's too hot today.
7. It's too cold today.
8. It's too wet today.
9. It's too dry today.
10. There's too much snow today.
11. There's not enough snow today.
12. There's a recession on.
13. There's a depression coming.
14. The sales manager doesn't know what he's doing.
15. The sales manager's an idiot.
16. The owner's an idiot.
17. The company's no good.
18. The products or services you're selling are no good.

19. And here's a classic: some salespeople be-
    lieve that selling is luck. When they miss
    a sale, they were just unlucky; when some-
    one else makes a sale, they were just lucky.
20. And another excuse that is just coming into
    vogue, one I think will be used for years
    to come, is the gas shortage or energy
    crunch.

I could go on and on. When you are not successful in your sales field, you are simply not using the
most effective methods. When you have mastered
the art of power and control selling, you won't need
excuses.

Chapter 5 told of the pressures of being a draw
or commission salesperson. You must realize the
pressures are self-made. When you understand this
fact, you can keep the pressures on, or you can take
them off. Here are some reasons you may feel intense pressure:

1. Your sales efforts are not effective enough.
2. You are not producing enough.
3. You are not making the kind of money you
   want or need.
4. You have little or no confidence in yourself.
5. You do not have enough control over yourself or your customers.

When you have one or more of these problems, you have pressure. I say unequivocally, the art of power and control selling will eliminate all the problems I have mentioned above. The equation is as follows: when the problems are gone, the pressure is gone.

What does it take to become a true professional in your business? Let's look at some of the specifics listed earlier in the chapter.

In what environment can you perform best and be most effective? John D. was born on a farm and grew up in a rural area. He moved to a metropolitan area at age twenty-three and went to work for a local automobile dealer in the heart of the inner city. John D. averaged about $14,000 a year. The percentage of the dealer's customers was broken up this way: 85 percent black, 15 percent white, Hispanic, etc. John was white and since he was born and raised on a farm, he didn't understand some of the black slang and streetwise talk that was a part of the black community. John found himself being called prejudiced when controversies arose with customers or other salesmen, the majority of whom were black. John D. also found that it was difficult or awkward to become a part of the immediate community by joining business, civic, or social groups.

Let's say that John D. read this book, *The Art*

of Power and Control Selling, and increased his earnings one hundred percent to $28,000. Would you say that John D. had become a true professional in his business? The answer is no. Even though John D.'s earnings have increased dramatically through the art of power and control selling, that is not enough. First of all, let me say there is no John D. This is a fictitious story and John D. is a hypothetical person. This situation is meant to show you there can be artificial barriers in the environment that can prohibit a salesperson from becoming a true professional in his business.

John D. could be a black salesperson selling in a white environment, or a person of Arabic descent selling in a Jewish environment. The answer is to make what you are work *for* you, instead of *against* you. If you know that you can get along better with one group of people than with others, let that work for you instead of against you. Do not put up with artificial barriers that cost you money and cut down on your effectiveness. These artificial barriers can be educational background, race, religion, or ethnic background; try and think of groups of people you work best with. The same is true with location: do you fit in and perform best in an urban, rural, semi-urban, or semi-rural environment, or anywhere in between? Find out the location and environment in which you can become a true professional in your business.

What product or service can you sell most effectively and successfully? I am going to make a statement that will probably shock half of you and make a lot of sense to the other half. Don't sell a product or service if a salesperson somewhere selling in the same capacity as you has not made a hundred thousand dollars a year selling the same thing. If, after a thorough examination of your product or service, you have not found or heard of a salesperson making one hundred thousand dollars in one year, drop it. Find a product or service to sell where the above is true, unless you are planning to be promoted to a job level in your company that has a potential of one hundred thousand dollars a year. When you have mastered the art of power and control selling, you will be successful no matter what product or service you sell. The whole idea is to make you as financially successful as possible. Some products or services have a greater profit potential for different individuals than others. *The Art of Power and Control Selling* will give you the blueprint for success in sales. I want you to find the product or service that has the greatest profit potential for you.

Is your company's method of doing business

best for you? By methods, I mean company rules, procedures, systems, laws, regulations, principles and standards.

All company rules may not be good rules.
All company procedures may not be good procedures.
All company systems may not be good systems.
All company laws may not be good laws.
All company regulations may not be good regulations.
All company principles may not be good principles.
And all company standards may not be good standards.

I am speaking strictly of how the above works for you as an individual. I must also clarify that what may be best for the company may not be comfortable for you. In discussing how to really become a true professional in your business, I want you to understand how company methods can vary from company to company. These methods can have a great effect upon achieving your goal of really becoming a true professional in your business. Understanding this can mean the difference between limited success and great success. My criterion for deciding whether a company's methods of doing business have a good effect or bad effect upon you is simple. My definition of good effects: if you are making the kind of money you want and are happy with your working environment, that's a good situation. If you master the art of power and control selling, that kind of a situation is very probable. Bad effects would be just the opposite of the above.

All the words I have used to describe a company's methods can vary from company to company. I am speaking of companies in the same business. Let's take five real estate companies. Even though they all sell the same thing—houses, residential, and commercial properties—the methods may vary from broker to broker. The reason for this is that smaller businesses seem to be an extension of the owner and somewhat reflect his or her character and belief. Breaking the same rule might call for dismissal at one office, but might only bring a casual comment at another. Larger sales organizations will reflect the character and methods of the sales manager or general manager, which means that each time there is a change of sales managers, district managers, regional managers, or general managers, there is usually a corresponding change in methods, again reflecting the character and beliefs of the people in charge.

A word or two about rules and procedures. Company rules could be anything from governing the length of hair to how many telephone calls you must make every day. All company rules are not good or fair. It is up to you to have a personal talk with one of the managers or the owner to express your feelings about any given rule. If you strongly feel that a given rule affects your performance, and the rule cannot be changed, think about changing companies. But, by the same token, if everybody else working in your same capacity is satisfied with the rule, this rule is good for the company, although it may not be good for you as an individual.

One would always like to see company procedures that are conducive to more business and better business. I'm sure all companies like to think they are using the most modern, most effective, and most successful business procedures, and in most cases, they are. How do these procedures affect you individually? I use the reasoning that all salespeople aren't as bright or as quick, or as effective, or for that matter, as slow as every other salesperson. What may be good for Joe may be bad for Bob. A procedure that Sue thinks is the greatest may be the pits for Mary. The moral here is to find out what procedures help you to become a true professional in your business. The reason I have not listed specific procedures is there are just too many, and they vary greatly from business to business.

Systems, for a company that sells a product or service, are the steps one goes through to sell a company's product or service. Some believe their salespeople must use their system. Some companies are so rigid in their application, they give you a word-for-word speech. You must follow this speech verbatim. Some companies want you to work from a general sales pitch or sales presentation. They expect you to stay within the framework of that presentation. Now that you have *The Art of Power and Control Selling,* which is the best and most effective sales technique for today's modern buyer? A company's system would then supply you the terminology used in that particular business. If a company insists that their system and only their system is to be used, and you find this line of thinking too confining, it's time to look around for another position.

We will discuss company laws and regulations together, since they are almost one in the same. Laws can be local, county, state, or federal. These laws govern thousands of products or services. I will not attempt to list the hundreds of laws or the thousands of products or services they affect. One could write a separate book on that subject alone. If any laws adversely affect your sales attitude or sales performance, I suggest you find another business where the laws governing that business— whether they are local, county, state, or federal—are palatable to you. Regulations have the same governing effect as laws, except they are handled by a regulatory agency. The penalties for regulations are administered differently. The advice would be the same as with laws. If they are not palatable, find another company in sales that is not affected by the regulations you dislike.

Principles usually involve a moral issue based upon an individual's character or upbringing. Principles in any business may vary anywhere from A to Z. Your personal scruples will determine how you perceive the way business is being carried on. Of course, I hope you are a person of high moral character and standards, and would not become involved in deceitful or fraudulent sales or business practices. If you are this kind of person and your company's ethics are not above reproach, I suggest you find a company whose business ethics and morals are satisfactory to you. For you, as an individual salesperson, to build a reputation that is solid and lasting, your company must reflect the same respectability.

While we are on the subject of principles and ethics, let's just call this "Hill's Law of Respectability" for lack of a better name: *"Thou Shall Not Lie to the Buyer."*

A good business reputation is built upon truth and honesty. This foundation, once built, will last for a long time. A sales presentation built on lies is like a house of cards; it cannot and will not stand. When you have mastered the art of power and control selling, you will never again need lies, deception, or half-truths. You will be able to look the buyer straight in the eye and command what you want him to do. Stick to the truth. This habit of telling the truth will spill over into your personal life. You will find the need to tell even a small lie no longer necessary or desirable. Remember, honest principles make you a better salesperson.

Standards are a legacy of goodwill that have endured during a company's lifetime. Of course, this can work both ways. Good standards breed goodwill. Bad standards breed ill will. You might ask, what do a company's standards have to do with you? Good standards or goodwill are tangible assets to which a company may attach a monetary value to be paid when and if that company is sold. So try and pick a company to work for that has exhibited good standards all of its business life. This factor can be a definite asset to you. By the same rule, a company whose standards have given it a reputation of ill will can adversely affect your sales performance.

Do the personalities of the people you work for and with (other salespeople, sales manager, district manager, etc.) help you become the best you can be? Simply stated, a company is a group of people working together—in our case, to sell and deliver products and services to the buying public. Everyone working for the company has a specific duty to perform. We hope everyone will perform to the best of his or her ability. I have simplified my definition of a company to focus on your relation with other salespeople, sales managers, district managers, regional managers, and owners. All of these people, regardless of their position with the company, are people with normal "people problems"—hang-ups, neuroses, idiosyncrasies, good points, bad points, and some just plain peculiar habits. From time to time, you must step back and analyze the people you work with and work for. Strive to find out if you are being adversely affected by any one particular personality. I have seen good salespeople whose potential has been cut up to 50 percent because these individuals are being adversely treated, usually by a person in a position of authority.

It is just human nature to like some people more than others. A person will pick his or her favorites because of their looks, their personality, their likability; in the case of the opposite sex, their sexuality. These decisions to like or dislike another person follow no known business or professional patterns, because they are strictly emotional decisions. These are just feelings. . . .

Mature-thinking business people make decisions

based upon business sense and logic. Some people you now work with and work for have not reached that state of business maturity yet. They make decisions based upon emotions and feelings. If you are ever confronted with a person of this type, bring it to his attention immediately. Do not allow this kind of immature or neurotic person the luxury of making you feel uncomfortable or miserable. *The Art of Power and Control Selling* will give you the self-assurance and confidence to stop that kind of situation in its tracks. Once the person or persons who can change the situation are notified, allow a reasonable period of time for a change to take place. If nothing is done in that time period, do not procrastinate. Leave and find a sales situation which is more to your liking.

By analyzing the specific situations I have talked about in this chapter, and acting on them accordingly, you will have come a long way in your quest to really become a true professional in your business. If you use *The Art of Power and Control Selling* as your sales bible, outstanding sales success can be yours.

7

How Good Can You Be?

This is a question that most of us have asked ourselves many times. What are the absolute limits of success that I can achieve? Is success limited by the length and breadth of my God-given talent and intelligence? My belief is that you are limited only by your own imagination and belief in yourself. Am I saying the art of power and control selling is a blank check that can be cashed when you have met certain requirements and criteria? No, I am not going quite that far. But I do believe that any amount of success you desire can be yours, if you make sure you do not set goals that are just humanly impossible, beyond total human reasoning and logic.

Once you have set out on a journey to find out how good you can be, you must have the vehicle to take you from where you are to where you want to be in your chosen sales profession. This vehicle is

The Art of Power and Control Selling. This vehicle is sound and solid. It will take you to your destination with power and control.

Just as with any endeavor, you must work hard and work smart. If I give you the tools to till the garden and the seeds to plant the garden, you must supply the labor to produce a productive harvest. You will also be supplied with the proper directions to carry out this task.

As you read this book, believe there is a new day dawning in your life. It is filled with so much power and control, it will turn your whole life around. Follow this program to the letter and you will have mental toughness that can break down steel barriers. You will have mental strength, the likes of which you have never experienced before. You will have control over others and over yourself. I am going to stop short of promising a Shangri-la for people in the sales profession. But I sincerely believe we will take you closer than you've ever hoped to get.

When the question comes to mind, "How good can I really be?" your answer to yourself should be, "I am going to be the best." I am going to repeat a statement that is very profound and very important. Here's the statement: "Successful selling is acting." I will repeat, successful selling is acting. In other words, selling is acting out a part successfully to influence someone to buy whatever you are selling. I will add another very important statement: successful selling depends upon what you say and how you say it. I know that statement sounds simple, but it can be the difference between success and failure. Your success with the art of power and control selling will depend upon using the words we have given you to say, and saying them just the way you are told to say them.

To clarify this line of thinking even further, let me give you an example. I am sure we have all seen actors on stage, in movies, and on TV. The actor's performance seems like reality. An actor's performance can make you laugh, make you cry, make you angry, make you sad, and make you happy. To the actor, it was just his job, a performance. In other words, he was only acting. The thing that made his acting so believable was what he said and the way he said it. The actor drew all of these different emotions from the audience just by what he said and how he said it.

When an actor first reads the script the first eight to ten times, he cannot make the words work for him. This is new and unfamiliar to him. But once the actor has rehearsed the script for weeks, sometimes months, he then begins to make the words work for him and he is able to get the results he desires. Compare yourselves with the actor. Many actors get so engrossed in the part they are playing, they lose their own identities and literally become the person they are portraying. For all intents and purposes, they are that person. You are now the actor who is picking up the script—*The Art of Power and Control Selling*—for the first time. The words will not work for you the first time, nor the second or third or the tenth time. But, just as the actor, you rehearse *The Art of Power and Control Selling* again, again, again, and again. You begin to make the words work for you. You begin to feel the power in your voice when you speak. You are speaking and commanding people with authority. The mental toughness begins to take hold. Barriers you could not overcome before begin to fall like matchsticks. You feel a surge of mental strength and power like a mighty dam about to burst. You begin to control people and situations with such ease you will almost think it's magic. This is it. This is what you have been working for. You have reached a new milestone in your life. Your professional sales life is starting to move with power and control. Ask yourself, "How good can I really be?" You repeat, loud and clear, "I am going to be the best."

The art of power and control selling is structured to give the greatest effect on what you say and how you say it. The art of power and control selling involves a great deal of human psychology. I will not pursue the psychological aspect of the art of power and control selling. To go into that phase would only complicate a book that I have intended to keep simple, easy to read, easy to understand, and easy to follow. The fact that it works is more impressive to me than all of the psychological jargon in the dictionary. Furthermore, I am not a qualified psychologist. I am a professional salesperson, just as most of you reading this book, who during 1978 made over $100,000. Ninety-five percent of the salesmen in my business, selling the same product, will not make half of that in a year.

I wrote this book because I felt we desperately needed a new and different method of dealing with today's modern buyer. I feel we are dealing with a buyer who is more confused than ever before, a buyer who feels more powerless than ever before, a buyer who feels more frustrated and feels he has less control over his destiny than ever before. This change started with the Korean War, followed by the Vietnam War, aided by the loss of faith in our government. Add to that, skyrocketing inflation, the gas shortage and energy crunch, and don't forget the recessions that seem to pop up every three or four years. Today's consumer is shocked and confused beyond belief.

You are in business for yourselves. A great many salespeople fail to realize that they are in business for themselves. Your employer provides you with the product or service to sell and a place to do business (usually a showroom and an office with desk and a phone, unless you are on the road). The company also provides you with the different printed matter that fits your particular business. This may include contracts, flyers, informational materials, booklets, samples, and any other items that are necessary for you to do business. What you do with the things you have to work with depends entirely upon you and you alone.

If you were to make a comparative examination of salespeople selling the same product or services for different companies in different states all over the country, you could compare paychecks by the week, by the month, or by the year and they would range anywhere along the pay scale from A to Z, even though they are selling the same product or service to the same kind of people. You are just like any other independent businessman whose income can fluctuate, depending upon how good a businessman the individual is. Your income depends upon what you, as an individual salesperson, can produce individually. You must change your thinking and philosophy about yourself and your role. You must stop thinking of yourself as "just" a salesperson. You are an independent business person who happens to be employed by a specific company selling a specific product or service. For example: any small store owner will work harder and longer hours because he is working for himself. He works harder because he has his own money invested, which can sometimes be his life savings. As a salesperson, you have your time invested—your most valuable asset. To a salesperson, time is money. You also have your future invested, which is life itself. When you waste time, let there be no doubt you are also wasting money. And, just as important, you are wasting your future and your life. So, no longer think of yourself as just a salesperson; think of yourself as an independent business person who sells. The amount of money you make depends upon you, not upon the company you represent, or the product or service you sell, but upon you as an independent business person. Remember, your financial success depends upon thinking like an independent business person, acting like an independent business person, and working like an independent business person.

Use *The Art of Power and Control Selling* as a map to find the highways to success, and keep asking yourself, "How good can I really be?" There is no doubt you are going to be the best.

BELIEVING IN YOURSELF

As I have said before, the field of professional selling is like the field of battle. If you are going to win, you must have the best and most efficient weapons available. Battles are won by having the best weapons or offense to overcome the enemy's defense. When you have this combination of circumstances, you are surely going to win. The only way you can lose is by not using the weapons at hand. The weapons you will need are provided here in *The Art of Power and Control Selling*. To be as good as you really can be, you have to believe in yourself. Believing in yourself is a part of the art of power and control selling.

Practice the procedures we tell you to practice. Rehearse the things we ask you to rehearse. Start by becoming mentally tough the way we ask you to do. Develop an authoritative voice that doesn't ask, but commands. Rehearse the lines until they feel as natural as the tongue in your mouth. Don't be afraid to feel the energy and power that are building up. Open up and let the energy and power surge through your body like bolts of lightning. Open up your mind and let the positive surge of mental energy brush aside all doubts and smash all indecision. You are going to be possessed by the art of power and control selling. It is truly a glorious and powerful feeling. I know some of you will ask, "Can I apply the principles in *The Art of Power and Control Selling* to my personal life?" The answer is yes. The reasons you do things in your business life are not the same reasons for action in your personal life, but the benefits in your nonbusiness life could be very positive.

First of all, your self-image and your inner feelings about yourself will become positive and powerful. You will begin to face nonbusiness situations and problems with a new feeling of confidence, power, and control that was not possible before. One-on-one situations that were a cause of fear, uneasiness, and even intimidation will be eradicated. You will draw from *The Art of Power and Control Selling* an authoritative manner, a commanding voice, a newfound mental toughness. You will move with an aura of absolute power and control. I don't mean to say that I want other people in your presence to feel uncomfortable or intimidated. The one word most appropriate to the feelings of people you meet will be respect. The procedures you learn in *The Art of Power and Control Selling* will make you a walking bundle of power. Your voice, your presence, your attitude all show POWER.

The information in the last paragraphs should be especially valuable and helpful to the timid, the shy, the meek, and the indecisive.

Again, we ask, "How good can I be?" Your answer, as always, "I am going to be the *best*."

8

How to Make the Telephone
a Dynamic Part of
Your Sales Image

I personally believe the telephone is one of the three greatest inventions in modern history. It is the salesperson's greatest tool. The telephone is the one device that has been responsible for closing more deals, making more money, creating more goodwill, and exchanging more ideas than anything else before or since its invention. There may be some invention on the horizon to surpass the telephone as a sales tool, but it has not come to light yet.

A great many salespeople have not taken advantage of this incomparable tool. Many think of the telephone as a device for staying in touch with family and friends, just a recreational gadget used to chitchat with friends and acquaintances, to pass the time of day, to catch up on the latest gossip—whether it be company gossip, industry gossip, or personal gossip. The gossip usually starts with the phrase, "Did you hear about so-and-so?" If I had a dime for every time that phrase was repeated in this country every day, I would be a rich man and could afford to retire for life. I have heard many people in sales say, "I'm just no good on the phone," or "I just can't be convincing on the phone." You will see the same person talking on the phone for an hour to a friend expressing every emotion under the sun, with voice modulations and facial expressions to match. I often have to laugh about that.

I say that anybody can learn to be positive, pleasant, and persuasive on the phone. Let's call this "Hill's Law of the Three P's."

The Art and Power of Control Selling teaches you to develop mental toughness. You will be able to break down mental barriers that heretofore you thought were unbreakable. This feeling gives you a positive attitude about yourself and whatever you do. Being positive will simply be a part of your personality. Your voice is being developed through our voice exercises to give it a positive tone. The qualities in your voice come through the phone just as if you were there. Therefore, having a positive attitude and a positive voice tone takes care of the first "P" in "Hill's Law."

Being pleasant on the phone is just as important as the other two "P's." A pleasant-sounding person gives the party at the other end a nice, warm feeling. It means the other party enjoys hearing your voice. Being pleasant on the phone causes the other party to be more receptive and open-minded about what you are saying. If this is a first call or contact, it makes that all-important first impression a good one that will carry over into other calls or a face-to-face meeting. If it is not the first call, it merely reinforces the good impression that was made with your first call or meeting.

If there is any doubt about how to sound pleasant, speak as if you were speaking to a really good friend or someone you care about. By always speaking this way on the phone, there will never be any doubt about sounding pleasant. That takes care of the second "P" in "Hill's Law."

Being persuasive on the phone is equally as important as the other two requisites. You have learned in *The Art of Power and Control Selling* to speak in a firm and authoritative voice. Don't just ask, but give commands. Just as the other party on the phone can feel your positive vibrations and the warmth from your pleasant personality, the other party can also feel the power and control your voice exerts. Being persuasive on the phone means you are able to plant a seed in the other party's mind. You can have him or her say yes about a product or service on the strength of what you say and how you say it. That's the third "P" in "Hill's Law of the Three P's."

Don't be afraid to pick up the phone and make calls. Just remember "Hill's Law of the Three P's." You will get to like using the phone more often. You will become a believer in what I have said earlier. The phone is the salesman's greatest tool.

I have seen people buy products or services right over the phone that they have never seen, used, or even heard of before they were called. I have seen everything from cars to magazines, carpets, home improvements, and raw land sold right over the phone.

Here's a phone pitch anyone can use, cold-calling for any product or service anywhere in the country. I will not specify a certain product or service, for there are simply too many. We all know that referrals (friends and relatives referring other friends and relatives) are not only the best and most qualified prospects but also the most profitable. Referrals provide an unending chain of prospects. The more referrals you get, the more referrals you're going to get. As you increase your customer base, you have more people to make referrals.

I have noticed many salesmen have problems prospecting. At this point, I would like to introduce what I shall call the "Magic Pitch." The reason for this name is that the results have been so fantastic.

This pitch is for cold-calling—out of the phone book or from any list you have available. The pitch is delivered over the phone and can be used in any business.

When you greet the prospect over the phone, put a smile in your voice. People like to talk to people who sound pleasant on the phone. Then say, "Mr. Prospect, I hear that you've been thinking about buying (whatever product or service your particular company handles) ." This question immediately accomplishes three things:

1. You speak in a very friendly and pleasing tone, and immediately seem to be a pleasant person.
2. The prospect feels that a friend or relative could have possibly referred him to you, and every salesperson knows that the customers he gets through referrals are the easiest to sell and the most profitable.
3. You do not annoy the prospect by trying to sell him something. You are merely asking him a question, which he will answer gladly.

If the prospect states that he has been thinking about buying your particular service or product, you immediately proceed to take whatever steps are necessary to close the sale.

If the prospect states that he has not been thinking about buying, you then ask him if it could have possibly been someone else in his family, or even one of his friends, who was interested.

Those two questions took the grand total of two minutes to ask. In those two minutes, you have touched three hundred, four hundred, possibly five hundred people—the prospect, his entire family, including sons, daughters, brothers, sisters, aunts, uncles, nieces, nephews, first cousins, second cousins, every possible relative, and all of his friends.

Even though simple to use, it works effectively. The results you can accomplish can seem truly magical.

In conclusion, I feel in coping with today's modern buyer you need the most modern and effective weapons that are available.

I trust you have found these weapons in *The Art of Power and Control Selling*, and with practice and perfection, you will become one of the outstanding salespeople in your field.

9

Grooming Tips
for the Successful Salesman

The Art of Power and Control Selling has given you the most effective weapons to conquer today's modern buyer. When you have practiced and rehearsed the procedures you have learned, you will have the finest and most effective weapons to enter into the arena of sales and come away victorious.

I am now going to talk about the physical side of successful selling. This includes your personal grooming habits and the attire you wear. The Gillette Safety Razor Company has a slogan that goes like this: "If you look sharp, you feel sharp." I believe in that statement implicitly. When a customer meets you in person, the way you're dressed and the way you're groomed go a long way to determine how the buyer perceives you. You've heard the saying, "First impressions are lasting." The art of power and control selling intends you to be as sharp mentally as any salesperson in the country. It would not make sense to have you so sharp mentally and not be sharp physically. To be the consummate success you want to become, you must be sharp physically as well as mentally. One enhances the other. We will offer tips on grooming. These tips on grooming and attire will not be difficult or expensive to achieve. It's really a matter of common sense, good hygiene habits, and buying outfits that match.

Some people are clotheshorses. That will not be necessary to look professional and well groomed. It's not what you wear, but the way you wear it. I'm sure we've noticed other people who always seem to look so well in whatever they wear. It might surprise you to find that some of these people spend less on clothes than you do. Some people just seem to have the knack for blending colors and shades better than others. People are not born with this trait, but you can learn their secret, too.

Let's start with suits. Vested suits are still the best bet for business wear because, even without the jacket, you still look dressed. With the jacket on, the suit has a neat continuity about it.

Do not get in the habit of buying cheap suits. First of all, it's hard to get a good professional fit. Second, the seams have a tendency not to stay together. Third, they wear out much more quickly. I know what you are thinking. At today's prices, even the cheap suits are expensive. I agree, but let me tell you about my experience in buying clothes. I have in my closets suits with names such as GGG, Petrocelli Eagles, King's Ridge, and such international designers as Yves St. Laurent, Adolpho, Francis Naurel, and Hardy Ames. All of these suits cost less than one hundred dollars apiece.

What's my secret? I have none. I wait until a fine men's store has a going-out-of-business sale, with prices up to 70 percent off retail. I buy five, six, or seven suits at a time. Get there early for a good selection of colors and sizes. The fit and feel of a fine garment gives one a sense of pride.

If no stores in your area are going out of business, check midyear or after-Christmas sales, which can offer up to 30 to 50 percent off. Try and buy at least three or more good suits when you catch a sale. Go early, don't wait until the last minute when everything is gone. Try to get there the first day and the first hour.

Pick suits that are not too flashy or gaudy; you don't want to look like you work for the circus. Pick colors such as dark or medium blues, charcoal or medium greys, dark or medium browns. A dark green or beige can add a little dash to your wardrobe.

Choose shirts that are white (preferably white on white) or a solid blue or beige to match a blue or beige suit. I am a great believer in white shirts for business; they have an air of class. Shirts should also be bought on sale and in quantity.

A solid-colored tie should be the same color as the suit, but in a contrasting shade. For example, a light brown tie with a dark suit (or vice versa) is an excellent combination. A tie that is multi-colored should have a color that matches the suit. For example, if you have a dark brown suit, the brown in the tie should match the suit as closely as possible, letting the other colors in the tie add contrast and flair. Ties should also be bought on sale or in going-out-of-business sales, in quantity.

Socks should always match the suit. Some fashion people will say the tie and the socks should match. I disagree. I like to see the lower pants leg blend with the socks, as if one. It is that line of continuity of color that brings about order in dress. For length, I prefer socks that go to the knee. Short socks are a no-no. Socks do not have to be bought on sale, since the average cost per pair is around two to three dollars. For every suit, have at least two pairs of matching socks.

Shoes are your foundation. I've always said, "Everybody should stand on a good foundation." My advice when buying shoes is to buy the best or nearly the best, because cheaper shoes wear out twice as fast, and they don't hold their shape. You might as well take the money for two cheaper pairs and buy one good pair. Every pair of shoes should match a suit. The shoes should have been bought to wear with that suit from the outset. The pants leg, socks, and shoes should be basically the same color, giving a clean line of color coordination. For example, brown pants leg, brown socks, brown shoes for a clean look. If you can wear a loafer or slip-on type shoe, it will give you a clean, neat look about the feet. Tie-up shoes are fine, too; I just prefer one to the other.

Personal grooming means care for your hair, your skin, your teeth, and your mustache.

Hair has gotten back to a reasonable length, which I personally have always liked. I believe you should keep your hair at a reasonable length, well trimmed and combed neatly. Collars are not hidden anymore, so let's make sure we see yours.

Skin is something most men have neglected. Recently, skin salons have begun to advertise. They cater to male customers for full-service skin treatments; some companies now have a complete line of skin conditioners. These products include moisturizers and masks for cleansing the skin, tighteners, etc. Since salons are rather expensive, your local drugstore, or a national chain such as Revco, Walgreen's, or Eckerd's will have products that could be helpful.

If you shave, make sure you are clean-shaven every day. It doesn't matter whether you use a safety razor or an electric. If your present razor is not getting the job done, experiment with different kinds of razors. Nicks and cuts are very unsightly. If this is a problem, try a different razor and blade.

Have your teeth as clean and as shiny as possible. Have your teeth cleaned by a dentist. Use the various tooth polishes and whiteners available at any drugstore. If you smoke, the nicotine tends to yellow your teeth. Keep a supply of tooth polish or whitener on hand.

Beards and mustaches should be neat and kept well trimmed. Neatness should be the order of the day.

I repeat, when you look sharp, you will feel sharp.

In closing this chapter, I must add some practical and pertinent information about dress in different areas of the country. If you are selling in a small rural area, you would not dress like a New York stockbroker, or vice versa. Instead of a suit, you might wear a regular pair of pants—nothing fancy—with a shirt open at the collar and no tie, a pair of good sturdy shoes or boots. In general you should reflect the commonly accepted dress styles of others around you. For instance, if you worked in Texas, even in the big cities, your business attire might be a suit with a cowboy flair, a pair of high-heeled cowboy boots, and a string tie—and you'd be at the height of fashion. Or if California is your home, your business dress in that informal atmosphere might be a sport shirt worn with sweater and slacks.

No matter in what area of this great country you may work or live, and no matter what dress styles are prevalent in your area, my tips about personal grooming, coordinating colors, and buying at going-out-of-business, midyear, or after-Christmas sales still hold true throughout the width and breadth of this country.